# Taxi stories from Finland

Over 100 funny and astonishing stories
by a local crazy cabbie

**Part One**

**Paul V. Speed**
**2015**

*All rights reserved.
Without limiting the rights under copyright reserved above, no part of this publication may be reproduced, stored in or introduced into a retrieval system or transmitted, in any form or by any means (electronic, mechanical, photocopying, recording or otherwise) without the prior written permission of both the copyright owner and the above publisher of this book.*

*© Paul V. Speed, 2015
All rights reserved
Publisher: Paul V. Speed
Translator: Little T
Copy editing: Native Speaker Llc*

The stories in this book are mainly my own experiences or fantasies about taxi driving. The events described here do not necessarily match the experience of other taxi drivers in any way.

For more stories, go to my blog:
https://lifeinfinlanddotnet.wordpress.com/

ACKNOWLEDGEMENTS

**Many thanks to supporters who helped me get this book published:**

Special thanks for a huge contribution to **Christopher B. Dodd.**

Likewise, special thanks for a great contribution to **Peeter Karm.**

A big thank you for your contribution goes out to **Katrin Lehtveer and Risto Sülluste, Tarmo Toomesoo.**

I dedicate this book to all the friendly, fun and polite customers I had the privilege of sharing a pleasant journey with in this life.

There are about 100 stories in this book. Not everything written here is true but it probably has happened or will happen.

For more stories, go to
https://lifeinfinlanddotnet.wordpress.com/

Many thanks to the translator, the editor and the designer for giving this book the good content and appearance it has.

I thank my friend Chubby and aunt K in Finland, they are the reason my life in Finland started. I also thank my friends in Estonia who motivated me to write these stories down. When the times were tough, your positive feedback gave me much strength and belief to continue writing this book.

Many thanks to my Finnish friends Heljä and Tapsa, they made all the photos in this book possible.

I also thank my other Finnish friends – Beard, who always offered us his "housing," his superb sauna, the blue and cold Hartwall "cartridges" and his great company, and Richard for the good Finnish humor and the "baked goods."

I thank my boss for the trust in me and the chance of having a job that expanded my way of looking at the world immensely. Thanks to this job I saw how colorful and diverse our world and the people in it can be. Thanks to these experiences I grew "bigger" myself.

I thank my colleagues, especially Lässi, Doggy and Tapsa – you were always helpful, kind, friendly and made the transition better with your entertaining and subtle Finnish humor.

And of course I thank my brother Teet for the unforgettable moments while driving as well as outside of work. We have things to remember.

*Paul*

# TABLE OF CONTENTS OF PART ONE

FROM THE BEGINNING ............................................. 9

BRIEFLY ABOUT CABBIES' JOB .......................... 11

BEGINNER'S SLIP-UPS ........................................... 16

COMEDIANS AND COMICAL FARES .................... 31

ARROGANT OR JUST STUPID? ............................ 66

SHIT-FACED CLOWNS .......................................... 109

FUNKY SENIORS ................................................... 211

ADVENTURES WITH YOUNGSTERS ................... 222

A COUPLE OF STORIES USHERING IN PART TWO OF THE BOOK ....................................................... 263

APPENDIX .............................................................. 275

WHICH IS IT – VIRO OR EESTI? .......................... 285

## TABLE OF CONTENTS OF BOOK PART TWO

### SEX, DRUGS, GUNS AND PSYCHOPATHS
Stories with sex, prostitutes, drugs, guns and aggressive people

### IT'S GOOD TO BE AN ESTONIAN
Pleasant and unpleasant stories involving Estonians

### PLEASANT AND UPLIFTING MOMENTS
Delightful drives with fun people that made me as well as the customer happy

### STORIES FROM AND WITH COLLEAGUES
Incidents told to me by colleagues

### HOLIDAYS
Some of the more interesting adventures that happened on holidays

### APPENDIX
### MORE USEFUL PHRASES IN FINNISH

## FROM THE BEGINNING

My younger brother called me on an evening in January and asked me if I would like to go work as a taxi driver in Finland. At first I didn't know what to say because I had never thought of myself as a taxi driver. I told him that I needed to think for a bit because I was already working in the construction business.

A couple weeks passed. I contacted the owner and manager of the taxi company directly. I informed him that I had to turn down his proposal this time. I decided to stay in the construction business. The owner understood and took my announcement really calmly. He wished me good luck and told me that if I ever needed a job I could turn to him.

Another 6 months passed. The project on my construction job had ended and I went on a holiday. I was also waiting for the next construction project. It was postponed several times. A couple of months had gone by since my last project. I was considering the proposal I had gotten from the taxi company.

I got in touch with the owner again. The gentleman, who had been working in the taxi business for about 30 years, was glad I contacted him. He promised he would arrange a training program for me and later hire me at his company. I was happy to still have an opportunity to get a job in the taxi business. Furthermore, I was already imagining myself driving a nice and expensive car, carrying around polite Finns. I envisioned that the job would just be fun, that I would meet cheerful people and earn money easily.

But to find out what really happened, keep on reading...

## BRIEFLY ABOUT CABBIES' JOB

The profession of a taxi driver is psychologically hard. Especially for the drivers who drive only on evenings and at night. Imagine a lifestyle of a taxi driver who only works at night. You usually wake up at 2-3 pm. You start your work or shift at about 4-5 pm. Then you drive for at least 12 hours from dusk to darkness and to dusk again. Of course only in summer, in autumn or in winter when you can barely see the sun in the northern climate, you just drive from darkness to darkness.

*1. The view on a main street in Helsinki city center.*

On almost all of these drives your travel companions are completely unknown citizens who you see for the first time. You have no idea what kind of person they are, what they are thinking about, what their intentions are and how they might react to something. And with these passengers you have to drive to unpredictable locations during EVERY round. Yes, most of the places you become familiar with, but you will not meet almost any of your customers ever again or you just forget that you have met them. Hundreds of different people go through your car and life in just months. And even if you see an "old acquaintance," you still don't know how the trip with him is going to be this time – maybe he's in a bad mood that day, maybe he is disturbed by the driver, meaning you. Maybe he had a bad day at work or maybe he hates the muddy, cold, depressing weather. And there is no point judging a customer by their appearance – looks are deceiving. I say this from my own experience. I have met very decently dressed people whose behavior has been terrible – some of them have been impolite, aggressive, some of them have unpaid bills on the home front. And I have met people who are dirty, sometimes in ragged clothes, who have been very polite, often leaving a tip and wishing the best after the drive. People are VERY different.

We all have certain types of people in our lives – people we like to or have to socialize with. But it's a limited crowd. A taxi driver must socialize with a huge number of people, whose character can vary in all kinds of ways. The behavior of people can often surprise you. The more you work, the less surprised you are...

There are many legends about taxi driving and taxi drivers– about mystical locations and mysterious happenings in the car, some of them tragic, unfortunately. I will not state my opinion about these stories. After reading this book, everyone can decide for themselves what is true and what is not.

Because there are thousands of taxi drivers, you can imagine how many of these and other stories have happened. We all have our adventures and stories. Something happens to us every day. Sometimes something special, other times something annoying and boring and not worth remembering. But sometimes things happen–things you want to write down to remember them later on. I tell about 100 stories in this book, most of them have happened to me and my colleagues working as a taxi driver in Finland. Mostly with Finnish people, but not only.

The Part One and Two contain tales about other nationalities – Estonians, Russians, Swedish, Americans, Germans, Jamaicans, Thais and others.

One thing that you, dear reader, should take from this book, is that I, as a person and a taxi driver, do not like people or customers who are loud, screaming, annoying or pick fights. I don't like people who can't be polite. I have not held back commenting on these kind of people in this book.

The events vary from pleasant and friendly drives with good people to very annoying drives. In the latter I will meet various people. Some have lost their minds drinking, some left without paying, and I needed to call the police on them.

I divided the stories into different chapters. I wrote them down in diary form, so there is a date next to every story. Then you can get a better idea of the situation.

Some chapters have more stories, some fewer. Some stories are longer than others, as is the time spent with the customers. Sometimes the drive can last half an hour but there might be nothing to write about if no action goes down during the trip. Sometimes it's the other way around. A fool might spend just 6-7 minutes in the car but you could write a whole page about the trip.

The book has been divided to different chapters by different moods, calls, events and passengers. Then you can easily choose what type of stories you want to read. Everything concerning the distances and costs is described in the metric system – meters, kilometers and euros.

The first stories took place when I started driving a taxi and chronicle events that happened because I wasn't familiar with the driving areas or the technology inside the car. There were funny and also nerve wracking moments when driving to a destination or in the payment stage.

The drives and the people who use the taxi are very different. The needs and purposes of different people in the taxi vary massively. But you can read about it in a minute. So get ready and fasten your seatbelt. It's going to be a hell of a ride!

## BEGINNER'S SLIP-UPS

A few stories from the beginning of my "career."

### First nights. Everything is new and unknown

My first night at work left an unforgettable impression because a snowstorm had just reached Finland. It was promising to be a tough night. In addition to the bad weather, I really didn't know my driving area, except some streets I had memorized in taxi driving school. I had no idea where they could be in real life, though. Even worse – I couldn't understand where the highways that connect different towns and neighborhoods were, or which other bigger roads they were connected to. On top of all that I was sitting in a car I hadn't even touched outside of a dealership – a Mercedes-Benz E-Class, sporty and comfortable as a cloud, worth about €50,000.

Oh yeah, I forgot to mention that all this swell equipment – GPS, meter, **Data**[1], plus all the standard features and extras on the car itself made me even more anxious.

---

[1] ***Data*** - *a device in taxis that displays info about the current fare/order.*

The GPS wasn't the most reliable. For one, it didn't function properly. Also, the maps in it were old and didn't show roads, streets or buildings built in the last few years. There are about 15,000 roads in Espoo, Helsinki and Vantaa combined.

2. A taxi stand in Helsinki city.

The most mysterious thing in the car was the meter. You can use it for all kinds of things. You can start a drive with various rates with it or you can enter "only" 49 different codes for a different bill. For example, if the customer has pre-ordered the taxi, you can enter a code to add the cost of the pre-order to the bill. Or if the customer needs help entering/exiting the car, or even getting in the house, you can add a **"helping tax"** to the bill. Or if you pick up a customer with two big Rottweilers, you can tax the transport of these kinds of beasts with an "extra cost for animals."

Anyway, the first night at work turned out to be really "fun." There was a lot of stress. Usually, the worse the weather, the more customers a taxi driver has, so there was a lot of work. In Finland, a taxi and a taxi driver are a part of the social safety net. If someone needs to go to the hospital, transport an old lady to a nursing home or "clean" a drunk citizen off the streets, they call a taxi.

The workload is especially heavy when the weather gets bad. People prefer taking a taxi to get from point A to point B, rather than driving themselves. They know it's much safer because taxi drivers are considered to be real professionals.

For the first few months I warned customers that I had just started my job. Actually I said that even after a few months. Right when they got in the car, I told them it would be better if they directed me where they want to go. That way we'd getto our destination without a hitch.

Most of the customers shared their knowledge gladly. A few of them just didn't know how to go where they were going so I had the chance to get to know new and exciting places with the customer.

### A drunk, panicking old lady and a "shared payment"

**November.** I picked up two older ladies and an older gentleman from **Espoonlahti**[2] at about 10 pm. Dressed respectably and well-spoken. They seemed to be Swedish, because I heard them talking in Swedish among themselves.

They wanted to go to **Kauniainen**[3], a small town about 13 kilometers north of **Espoo**[4]. *Oh, good, a de-*

---

[2]***Espoonlahti*** *– a district in the southwestern part of Espoo. It is located about 18km west of Helsinki.*
[3]***Kauniainen*** *– a small garden city just next to Espoo. It is located about 18km southwest of Helsinki.*
[4]***Espoo*** *– one of the biggest cities in southern Finland.*

*cent fare and a good addition to the cash register,* I was thinking to myself.

We arrived at Kauniainen without any problems. One of the ladies wished to exit the car when we got to her house. After she had left, the old couple in the car told me they wanted to go to **Martinlaakso**[5] district, in **Vantaa**[6] (about 17 kilometers northeast). I hadn't heard of that place before.

The gentleman gave me the address, I entered in the GPS and took off. After about 5 minutes of driving, it turned out that we had a little problem. The old couple wanted to take shortcuts and drive on the smaller roads. The GPS showed me the faster routes – on the bigger highways and motorways. So I trusted the GPS and we took the bigger roads.

Well, the couple was a bit drunk, the woman more than the man. During the trip, the woman in the backseat started to moan that we're driving in circles and that they should be home already. Yes, I missed a turn, but right away I paused the meter and let the gentleman, who was sitting next to me, know. I asked

---

[5]***Martinlaakso*** *– A district of Vantaa. It is located about 16km north of Helsinki.*

[6]***Vantaa****- City of Vantaa. It is located about 20km north of Helsinki.* ***Helsinki-Vantaa International Airport*** *is also located there.*

for his help and directions where he would like for me to drive. The mellow and chatty gentleman had no problem with that and offered his help. He directed us back on the right route and the journey went on as the meter ticked.

The lady in the back still wasn't happy about things and continued to cry in the backseat. She then moaned: "Fuck this, I'm not paying for the ride!" and that she would complain about me to the calling center.

I then politely and calmly tried to explain that if the drive was long and there were thousands of streets, there were many ways to the destination. And maybe she could forgive me, because it was the third night as a cabbie for me and I didn't know shit about how I could get from one place to another.

The granny in the back still couldn't get off the carousel and kept adding fuel to the fire. I thought it would be better not to argue, explain or apologize to a dumb person. It all seemed useless to me. I just smirked to myself and ignored the woman. Surprisingly, the man next to me had had it and yelled to her: "Hey, that's enough! We're going to get home in a bit, take a few shots, you'll calm down right away." I had a tough time holding my laugh back at that and the man started laughing himself.

We managed to arrive without further problems, the lady still moaning to herself.

I stopped next to the couple's house on the street. The gentleman thanked me for the ride and started to pay. I asked if the price was okay and if everything was fine.

Then we had another little surprise. The day before, during my round, the printer had run out of paper so I asked Teet to show me how to change it. But instead of showing me, he just changed it. Now, if I tried to print the receipt, no text would appear on the paper. He had put it in backwards. "Fuck, this is just what I need," I thought to myself when I saw the blank paper. Already, the chicken had been clucking in the back during the whole trip, how she would complain about me. Now this shit.

The drunk chicken had gotten out of the car and was now standing on the sidewalk with her "wings" on her hips, trying to be important. Of course she kept moaning how unsatisfied she was with everything.

The gentleman kept his calm. We were thinking what to do – I needed to give the receipt to them somehow.

So I called my boss, explaining the problem I had and asking for advice. He just mumbled something on the phone. I then came up with the idea to take the customer's information and that the boss would send the receipt to them later. That's what we decided to do.

In the meantime, someone had approached the car. It was a guy who had too much to drink. He had a croaky voice and wrinkly face. He had his girlfriend with him. They asked if I'm free. I looked the guy into his eyes and asked, "Don't you see I still have a fare?" He then pulled back and took a different approach and mumbled: "B-but..after you deal with th-them, *hic*, are you f-free then??"To that I told him: "Yes, then I'm free, but you need to wait. I have a little situation here." He then took a few more steps back, saying "Y-yeah, t-take your t-time, w-we got p-plenty of it."

After I finished talking with my boss and the drunk guy, I explained to the gentleman who had been my customer that the receipt would be later sent to him by mail. He was okay with that. He thanked me again and we went our different ways wishing each other a good evening.

Right then and there, I picked up the couple who had approached me. The drive was going to be about 2-3 kilometers. I was okay with that. I didn't even ask for the destination, I just had them direct me the right way. They agreed with that.

A few kilometers later the young lady wanted to stop and leave. And she wanted to pay for her part of the bill. Really?! I asked her "Can't your friend pay the 10 euros for you at the end of the fare?" "No. I want to pay for myself and right now," she answered. I then asked if she could pay with cash and must she really pay with a card? "No can do, I want to pay with my card," the chick said.

The dude in the backseat then decided to join our conversation and started to teach me: "Okay, now enter the code, enter the card, do this, do that and the bill is ready." I was surprised and asked him how the hell he knew that. He explained that he was a taxi driver himself.

The girl exited the car and we kept going with my newfound colleague, until we arrived near a bar. He paid the bill and went his way, I pulled off the street into someone's driveway to investigate what the hell was going on with the printer and the paper. Just as I was changing the roll and making sure it was the right way, a police bus stopped behind me. They watched my back until I got a new fare and drove to get the customer.

### The angry Swedish old lady

Talking about Swedish old ladies, one afternoon in **December**, I picked up an old lady from **Westend[7], southeast Espoo.** Westend is a district where the bold and the beautiful live in their big and fancy mansions.

Arriving at the lady's house and seeing her exit it, I exited the car. I opened the passenger door for her, set her seat in the right position and helped her sit in the car.

She wanted to drive to **Helsinki**, near a church. Before that, though, she wanted to go to **Ruoholahti[8], southwest Helsinki**, to her granddaughter's apartment to pick her up.

So we arrived in Helsinki. The GPS directed me to stay in the left lane and stay on the highway, not take the exit on the right to Ruoholahti. The lady said we should take the exit but wasn't sure.

---

[7]*Westend - a suburb district in the southeast part of Espoo next to Tapiola. It is located about 10km west of Helsinki.*
[8]*Ruoholahti - a district of Helsinki. It is located right near Länsisatama/ West Harbour.*

3. A small dock in Westend.

I kept going on the highway until it ended and asked the lady if she knows if should I turn left or right. The GPS still directed me left, to the center of the town. The woman answered the question with a serious and an important face, that she didn't know, but the place she wanted to go was not on the left.

I decided to follow the GPS and turned left. To that, the broad started yelling and lecturing me: "Where are you going, do you even know?" She kept abusing me: "How did they even let you behind the wheel of a taxi? I am going to complain to the calling center, that you can't find the destination!" That wasn't all. She told me that she would not go on with me and insisted that I'd stop right there.

I turned off into a bus stop on my left. I stopped the car and "paused" the meter. I was thinking if I should listen to the screaming woman or keep driving according to the GPS.

I decided to keep driving but the shouting got even louder. I then thought it would be safer to stop the car again and decide together with the lady how should we continue.

There was no point talking to her rationally. She just kept shouting, "You won't drive anywhere! I'll call my granddaughter and then we'll know where the hell we are." She was out of her mind.

In the meantime I called my boss. I asked him if maybe he could explain how I could get from where we were to where we needed to be. There was no hope, the shouting in my passenger seat was louder than anything I heard on the phone: "Hey, no talking on the phone! You won't go anywhere until my granddaughter gets here! You're a fucking idiot!" Yes, that's what she said.

My boss managed to explain to me that actually I was in the right place. I just needed to drive about 100 meters, then turn right and take another right. But she didn't give a shit. I ended the call with my boss and stayed in the car, waiting for her granddaughter during rush hour in a bus stop.

I looked at the passing traffic and thought to myself, how could a decent old lady flip out like this? I kept comforting myself that her behavior must be an exception and that this wasn't regular in this line of work. I had never met a Finnish person who had been this impolite. As it later turned out, I was wrong.

Anyway, about 6-7 minutes later, the grumpy lady's cheerful pretty granddaughter arrived and directed us to the correct church.

The hag offered me 20 euros for the fare, because that was the number on the meter when we were at the bus stop. I told her that it wasn't necessary. I did her a good deed – brought her to the church for free, accompanied by her shouting. She then instantly calmed down, thanked me and left the car, smiling.

I wasn't as thrilled by the trip. It was my first "empty drive." I returned to Westend to look for new fares.

### Nuottaniementie and Nuottamiehentie

On a midnight in **December** I had a passenger in **Matinkylä**[9]**, southern Espoo,** in **Nuottaniemi**[10] district, to a house on Nuottamiehentie street.

I was tired and read it as Nuotta*niemen*tie, where I had been several times before. A creature of habit.

So I turned to a familiar street, pulled up to a familiar house, parked the car, called the passenger and announced, satisfied with myself: "Hello, your taxi has arrived." The customer answered: "Hi, I'm outside too but I don't see a taxi." I explained that I was right in front of the house and confirmed the number of the house, just in case. "Yes, the number is right but I don't see any taxis on the street," the customer told me. I was wondering what the fuck was going on. I asked the customer what street he was on. He told me: "I'm standing on Nuottamiehentie." I looked at the GPS to see where I was. Shit!I was on Nuottaniementie, not Nuottamiehentie.

---

[9]***Matinkylä*** *– a fast developing district of Espoo located about 14km west of Helsinki.*
[10]***Nuottaniemi*** *- a district of private houses in Espoo, next to Matinkylä. It is located about 15km west of Helsinki.*

Fortunately, the mistake was only about 500 meters. I apologized to the customer and promised to be there in a few minutes. I then repeated to myself: "Focus, focus, focus and open your fucking eyes when reading an address!"

## COMEDIANS AND COMICAL FARES

### A trip to Jamppa[11] with the doppelganger of Bob Marley

About half past three on an early morning in **February** I got a call from a multi-story house in **Espoonlahti**. I thought it might be an old couple who were visiting someone and now wanted to go home, somewhere in **Helsinki**.

So I drove to the right address, arrived in front of the house. I looked for the right doorway to pick up the customer. In about a minute a fellow came out of the house and go into the backseat of my car. Slightly tipsy of course, but mellow and friendly. He looked like the famous reggae star Bob Marley, with real long dreadlocks. A woolen "sock" on his head like Jamaicans wear.

So I asked him where we would be headed. "To **Järvenpää**[12]," was the answer. I asked again because I thought I heard him wrong: "To where?!" "To Järvenpää," was the clear-cut response.

---

[11]*Jamppa* – *a district of town Järvenpää. It's located about 40km north of Helsinki center.*
[12]*Järvenpää* – *a city of about 40 000 people located 40km north of Helsinki.*

Shit, I approximately knew where it was on the map but I had no idea how to get there.

So I asked Bob a question only a novice would: "What area is it in, **Vantaa** or **Vihti**[13]?" The dude responded with: "Nonono, it's a separate place – Järvenpää. It's further than Vantaa, **Kerava**[14] or even **Sipoo**[15]." Hearing that, I thought, "Holy fuck, where in the hell do I have to drive this early morning. This is a really long drive." I had never had this long a fare.

So off we went. Me, desperately trying to find the address the guy told me. I didn't. Once more, I asked him for the street he wanted to go. "…street," (about 64km) the Bob Marley-like answer sounded. *Shiiit, you fit right in on that street*, I thought, hearing the street name again. Bob added that we could get there through **Lahdenväylä**[16] highway.

---

[13]*Vihti* - a parish in southern Finland located about 50km northwest of Helsinki.

[14]*Kerava* – a town in southern Finland located about 30km north-east of Helsinki.

[15]*Sipoo* - a parish in South-Finland located about 35km north-east of Helsinki.

[16]*Lahdenväylä* – about 100km long multilane highway from Helsinki heading northeast to the city of Lahti.

On the **Kehä I**[17] circuit, I was still looking for the Järvenpää address and still could not find it. Again, a completely fucked situation in the early morning. I would like to "thank" my GPS with its "mega-giga-new" maps.

Finally a light bulb turned on above my head. I entered the address of where I previously lived in **Lahti**[18], when I was working there. Okay. It worked. It showed me that we are going the right way and there would soon be an exit towards Lahti. At the same time I was not sure that everything would go as planned.

I pulled out an atlas from between the seats during the drive, browsing through the pages doing 80 in snowy weather. I tried to find where this fucking Järvenpää was and how to get there.

Finally I saw something on the map. There is a district called Jamppa in Järvenpää. Sure. Great name for a place. That's the place all the ganja-men must be isolated in Finland, I smirked.

---

[17]*Kehä I –the first and oldest circuit connecting Espoo and Itäkeskus, a district of East-Helsinki.*
[18]*Lahti – a city and municipality in Finland. It is situated on a bay at the southern end of lake Vesijärvi about 100 km northeast of the capital Helsinki. In English, the Finnish word Lahti means bay.*

So I pulled over on the Kehä I. I tried finding the address again and this time I succeeded. Woohoo! Now we could continue.

I stepped on the gas, driving towards Lahdenväylä. I looked in the rear-view mirror and saw that the dude was happy with the situation himself. At the same time I was thinking to myself, why the fuck should he take a drive this long at this kind of time. Suspicious.

I looked at the GPS, there was about 42kmto go – the bill was going to be huge. I started to doubt if he would pay. Would he try to run, or might something more interesting happen during the trip? Different scenarios were rolling in my head.

So just to check, I asked him, "Hey, sorry for asking but why are you a trip so expensive so early in the morning?" He responded: "The wife is waiting and I have to go home. I just stayed out too late and didn't get home earlier." "Okay," and I added, "Must be quite a wife if you're willing to take this kind of a trip." He answered, "Sometimes she is, yeah."

I turned towards Lahdenväylä and heard the dude doing something in the backseat. I couldn't see shit in the rear-view mirror because the lights had just ended on the motorway. It was pitch-black.

Again, I was thinking to myself, Damn, seems like things are getting interesting. If there's any bullshit, I will just hit the snow wall doing 100-110 and then see how things go. That was my masterplan.

The action in the backseat ended. I looked back over my shoulder to see what was going on. I saw the dude sleeping, head on his chest. Okay, cool. Another question was spinning in my head: "I wonder if he has money or will he say that he doesn't have any and run, so I have to deal with the police again."

I kept checking the rear-view mirror and saw him waking up and checking if we were going the right way. We were.

At last we arrived at his house. He started to pay the bill. He entered the wrong PIN number on his first try. *Fuck this, don't you fucking start this bullshit again*, I thought based on my previous experiences. He even asked if he could pay without entering his PIN. I told him I couldn't do that, although really I could have.

I re-entered his card into the reader and gave it to him to enter his PIN number. It worked. 106 euros, my biggest receipt was printing. I was relieved to get the money for the drive. The dude thanked me and started walking to his house to his wife. I drove a bit further to change the tape for the receipts, which had just run out.

I decided to take a smoke break and call my partner before driving back. I told him that I would be about half an hour late for the car-switch. I explained to him that I happened to be very far from home. 66kmof road was waiting on the drive back.

## An error by the dispatcher giving me the address. A drive like in an armored car

On the same evening in **March**, when we cleaned my car's front window with hot water with a Finnish worker in **Saunalahti**[19], **southwest Espoo**, I got a new fare after driving the worker to **Helsinki**.

Because the weather had turned into a snowstorm, I decided to drive to **Westend, Espoo** through the city center of Helsinki. I was hoping I could get some customers who didn't want to walk in this kind of shitty weather.

Right in the heart of the city, near the main train depot, I got a fare on Data showing an order on **Oikotie** street. After gliding on the extremely slippery,

---

[19]*Saunalahti - a new, developing district in the city of Espoo.*

snow-filled narrow cobblestoned streets of Helsinki, I finally reached the destination showed by Data.

The address of the house was Oikotie... D. But the house I arrived at only had two doorways – A and B. So I called the phone number shown in the order to ask the customer, how to get to the D doorway. As it turned out, I was in the wrong place! The right address was actually **Oikokatu**, which was over 3 km away. Of course I was cursing to myself: "Fucking calling center! How the hell can you make a mistake this big? It's really fun to drive an extra 3km in this kind of weather and to let the customer wait." I was afraid the customer would refuse the order and take another taxi. Fortunately, the customer was understanding and patient, saying he would wait for me.

So I tried to leave the Oikotie house, but its yard was filled with black ice. As my Merc was rear-wheel drive, it just drifted to the side but didn't move anywhere in these conditions. I nearly hit a garage door to the right of me.

After 4-5 tries, I managed to leave the ice-filled "bowl" without damaging the car and got to the right address. On the corner of the street, there was a young guy waiting for me. I apologized for taking so long and said the calling center had made an error.

Luckily, the dude was in a good mood and was happy he even got a taxi in this weather.

We drove to pick up a friend of his, to later take them drinking somewhere.

The destination, a burger joint, was about 6-7km away. Arriving there, it turned out that there were 2 friends instead of one.

We picked up his friends and had to drive back to the city center. It turned out to be an adventurous trip, because consuming alcohol in a car in winter wasn't the best idea, especially in the conditions that we had. The alcohol they breathed out froze all of the windows from the inside. Like that wasn't bad, the snowstorm kept filling the windows from the outside. Add all of that together and you have a situation where the wipers were just wiping dry ice on the window and visibility was almost none. The windscreen was completely frozen and snow falling on it didn't make it any better. Also, thanks to the humidity and alcohol in the air, the windows were completely fogged.

The visibility through the frozen front window was like driving a Russian armored car and looking out of the hatch. I managed to carve a hole in the ice about the size of my hand so I could see where I was going and what I could hit. A few times, when we were stopped by traffic lights, I got out of the car and bang the ice off the wipers. But it was no use. They were instantly covered in snow, as was the window, and the whole combination was again frozen to the window. I didn't receive any help using the heaters in the car or on the window – zero effect. Of course I was practically going berserk because of the quality of the car and the tiring drive.

All of the unpleasant conditions you could have, we did have – foggy, frozen windows, zero visibility, snow filled streets and roads like a skating rink.

At last, after about 15 minutes of "sweating," we arrived at the destination. The trio exited the car and I parked myself to a bus stop to have a calming cigarette and to let the car melt a bit. That didn't really work because it was still snowing.

And as long as it was snowing, the windows kept freezing and I kept ruining my nerves driving in complete invisibility. Several customers told me: "Hey, maybe you can clean the wipers." I demonstrated the practicality of that a couple of times.

The problem was that the window heaters were outside of the car, under the edge of the hood. They had been filled with snow and frozen. Finally, when the snowfall decreased a bit, I managed to clean the heaters properly. After that, the car looked more presentable from the outside as well as the inside and I could get from point A to point B with a bit less stress.

## Two "decent" pilots

**March.** I get a fare from a bar **Westend** at about 11 pm.

I drove to the bar and two guys entered the car, both in their 50s. One looked like the former Finnish ski jumping talent **Matti Nykänen**[20]. The other one was a look-alike of a well-known Estonian actor, **Lembit Ulfsak**[21]. When I looked at the first guy and heard him talk, I thought, it can't be Matti, touring around from bar to bar.

---

[20]*Matti Nykänen - is a Finnish former ski jumper who won five Olympic medals (four gold), nine World Championships medals (five gold) and 22 Finnish Championships medals (13 gold).*
*Since the 1990s, his status as a celebrity has mainly been fueled, not by his sporting achievements, but instead by his colorful personal relationships, his career as a singer, and various incidents often related to heavy use of alcohol and violent behavior. He was sentenced to jail for 26 months following a stabbing incident in 2004, and again for 16 months after aggravated assault on his wife in 2009.*

[21]*Lembit Ulfsak - is a prominent Estonian stage and film actor. Ulfsak stars in the 2014 foreign film Tangerines which has been nominated for the Best Foreign Language Film at the 87th Academy Awards. It was also among the five nominated films at the 72nd Golden Globe Awards for best foreign language film.*

The doppelganger of Matti wanted to go **Hauki-lahti**[22] (about 1km) and I needed to take the copy of Lembit to the border of **Espoo-Helsinki, Lauttasaari**[23], Vattuniemenkuja street. Can you imagine hearing that street name from a man drunk as a skunk? "Waddddunyiieeemenguyaaaa."

Long story short, I heard the first part of the name, but the end, "kuja", I didn't.

I found Vattuniemenkatu on the GPS and reached the highway when I noticed that Lembit next to me was sleeping. I told him "Hey, don't fall asleep, I'm not sure which house is yours. I don't know where to stop." Nothing. The sponge had soaked up too much alcohol and couldn't wake up.

I arrived on Vattuniementakatu and saw a house whose number was 13. I stopped the car and tried to wake the guy up. First talking quietly, then louder and louder. Finally I yelled and hit his shoulder: "Wake the fuck up!" Still nothing. It was no use.

I thought what to do. Then I remembered that cold air would help. I rolled down all the windows and went

---

[22]*Haukilahti* – *a district in the southern part of Espoo, mostly filled with multy-store houses. It is located about 12km west of Helsinki.*

[23]*Lauttasaari* – *an island with a district of Helsinki on it. Located about 5km west of the city center.*

about 70km/h on that same street. At the same time I kept working on him verbally and physically.

At the end of the street he came out of his unconsciousness. I stopped the car and yelled at him with the voice of a bear: "WHERE THE FUCK IS YOUR HOUSE??!!" He looked around and was astonished by the scenery. He didn't know where the fuck he was. First he pointed to a yard and then "Shit, that isn't it." He asked, "Where are we?" I loudly explained to him: "You are in LAUTTASAARI!" Several times.For fuck's sake.

So I kept driving down the street until we reached a store that the sponge recognized. "Oh, turn right here and take another right. And I said KUJA," the wise-ass told me. "You didn't say fucking anything understandable. You're lucky I understood which street you want to go to. It's a little difficult to figure out which language you're speaking today!"

I had stopped the meter by then. So I drove 400-500m around the corner, where his house was, for free. He told me he was *"ihan tyytyväinen, että pääsi perille*"[24]. That's exactly what he told me. He was very satisfied to get home.

The payment took time, because while he was looking for his card from his wallet, someone called him. He then started to moan that he was lost and something about being robbed. What a fucking idiot!

At the same time he was holding his phone in one hand, he had his card in his other hand. I snapped it from him and put it in the card reader to get rid of him quickly.

After he finished his call, he took just three tries to enter his PIN and I finally got my money for the "joyride." Then he started thanking me again and again for bringing him home. I finally told him "Hey, please leave the car now please. Another customer is waiting," because I had gotten another fare.

I finally got rid of him and drove to pick up a cute blonde lady and her dog who wanted to go to a little town called **Kauniainen** within Espoo. After wrestling with Lembit and Matti, a fare this easy was just what I needed.

---

[24] *"ihan tyytyväinen, että pääsi perille"* – *in English "really delightful for reaching his destination".*

## Like a canoe had been thrown on the wall of snow

**March. Espoo, Olari[25] taxi stand.**

I was the first taxi when I arrived at the stand. I saw a guy, about 22-23 years old, standing at the taxi stand, a bit more drunk than you would like. He entered my car and got on the front seat and told me: "Drive to that corner," showing me a bend about 30m away, where another bar was.

Shit, I thought he was playing a stupid joke on me and just wanted to drive 30 meters. Another damn moron trying to act cool. I got pissed off. I yelled at him: "Fucking walk, it's right there! Why the fuck should I leave my post to drive you 30 meters?" The guy was startled and told me: "No-no, my friends are coming out of the bar and joining us in a minute." "Oh, got it. I'm sorry, that's another story." I apologized, embarrassed. I reacted too quickly. The last fare with some drunk idiots was still in the back of my head.

I drove to the corner and in a few minutes, the friends arrived.

---

[25] *Olari - a district in the southern part of Espoo next to Matinkylä. It is located about 14km west of Helsinki.*

We drove to **Matinkylä** (about 1.5km). The guys were satisfied to even get a taxi. The two friends who had been picked up were amazed that their friend got a taxi so quickly when there was a shortage of cabs.

So the guys exited the car in a street in Matinkylä and I started to turn the car around.

I watched as the guys crossed the street. They had to go over a wall of snow of about 1 meter (about 3 feet). The alcohol had done its job; so had the cold weather with the street. Nature claimed another victim on that slippery wall of snow – one of the guys who started to go over the wall fell on his stomach, two hands to the side. He didn't get a chance to even defend himself with his arms. With his face down and ass up, the first image that popped into my mind was that a canoe had been plopped down on the wall of snow. I started laughing uncontrollably, as did the guys on the street. I was just hoping he didn't injure his face and that he was okay. I think he was, though. The guys didn't ask for my help. So I left their company in the good mood that I was in.

## Helsinki's midnight skier

On a weekend in **March**, when I had dropped off a customer in Helsinki, I turned back to go to **Westend, Espoo**. About 400 meters before turning on the highway, in the city center, near the **Kamppi**[26] shopping center, someone with skis was waving to me!

I stopped the car. We put his gear between the two seats so that one tip of the skis was touching the ceiling above the rear seat and the other was practically touching the buttons on the radio. I was lucky to have a car with automatic transmission, otherwise it would have been complicated to change gears.

Dude was a bit drunk too – it's the weekend, what are you going to expect. I asked him, "Did you go skiing in this time of night?!" He pointed to the right, out on the bay, as we had turned on to the highway and said: "Yeah, on that bay. There's a good track there." I asked more: "How many kilometers did you ski?" "Well about 10," the local skier answered. That ended our conversation.

---

[26] *Kamppi – a complex in the city center of Helsinki. It contains a bus station, metro station and many places for shopping. It took 4.5 years to build and it is visited by 700,000 people every week.*

When we arrived in **Haukilahti, southern Espoo**, where he wanted to go through **Niittykumppu**[27], McDonald's, he started to tell me on the highway that he wanted to get out. I asked, "Right here, in the middle of the highway?" "Well yeah, wherever you can stop."

"Wait, I thought you wanted to go to a McDonald's first?"

"No, I would like to stop right now," the dude answered.

Well what do you know? In the middle of a 4-5 lane highway, in the middle of the night, the guy wants to exit.

I turned off the highway towards **Nittykumppu** district. I told the guy: "I could stop right here, there's an intersection right here," as I was slowing down. I asked again just in case: "Is this spot okay?" "Umm, no-no, keep driving," the Ski King thought. I asked to specify: "Where to, towards the McDonald's?" "Well yeah, just keep driving, I'll tell you when to stop," the guy said in a groaning tone. It looked like the warm air had gotten to him, adding to the alcohol.

---

[27]*Niittykumppu – a district of Suur-Tapiola, in the part of southeast part of Espoo. It is located about 11km west of Helsinki.*

In about a minute we arrived at the McDonald's. The guy suddenly announced: "Stop the car now!" So I did. The skier paid the bill, took his gear and we parted our ways. I guess he had a specific budget for the taxi, which he held on to like the German minister of finance does with Germany's budget.

## A drunken clown and a tired foreigner

**April.** It was just half past midnight on a weekday. I was sitting at a taxi stand in **Tapiola[28], southeast Espoo**, when I got an order from a hotel nearby.

A gentleman in a suit, speaking in English, got on the ride. He looked pretty tired. You could tell he was actually fatigued in addition to the alcohol intoxication.

The gentleman wanted to go to **Itäkeskus[29]** east of **Helsinki** (about 23km). Before we got moving, some drunk Finnish clown jumped in the front seat and told me that we could start driving. I looked at him, surprised. I then looked at the gentleman in the back, as if to ask if he knew the man in the front. It turned out he did. The clown explained that he need-

---

[28]*Tapiola* – *a district of southeast Espoo, which contains a culture center. It is located about 9km west of Helsinki.*
[29]*Itäkeskus* – *a district in East-Helsinki located about 11km east of the city center.*

ed to talk to his friend, not wondering if the friend wanted to communicate with his Finnish companion.

I asked the Finn if he was going to the same place as his friend. "Yeah-yeah, we're going to a bar in Helsinki," he assured me in complete confidence. He didn't specify which one, though. The friend was sitting in the back, looking out the window, uninterested. He didn't seem to be particularly excited about the idea of the Finn, whose motor was running on alcohol.

The Finn started to summarize some meeting, which turned out to be a monologue. The English-speaking friend just nodded and answered yes to everything. The questions and statements which were complaints about their colleagues, he just ignored. It seemed like the Finn was hoping the foreigner would support his bitching.

On the Kehä I circuit, near the exit to **Haaga**[30], when we had been driving for about 10km, during a discussion between the two, it turned out the foreigner didn't want to go to a bar with the Finn. He wanted to go home and rest. The Finn seemed disappointed of course. Then he realized he was going the wrong

---

[30]*Haaga* – *a district of Helsinki. It is divided into 4 parts: South-Haaga, North-Haaga, Kivihaka and Lassila. It is located about 8km north of the city center.*

way. He told me right away that instead of going east, he needed to go west, to **Kirkkonummi**[31] (about 35km).

I asked him: "How are we going to solve this problem? Do I let you off here and you get another taxi for yourself?" "Nooo, could you call for another taxi yourself," the suddenly worried Finn asked. I told him, "Sure I could, but we need to find a place a bit more populated. I can't leave you in a random bus stop on Kehä I in the middle of the night." I kept explaining: "First, no taxi driver could find you here and second, you could venture somewhere. I'm to blame for letting you roam free if something happens."

After finishing my explanation, I took the next exit to **Pakila**[32] and turned left to a gas station. I was hoping it would be open and I could call a taxi for the clown there, so I could continue the trip with my other customer.

Shit, of course it was closed. Most of them close at 11pm-12am. It was already 1am.

---

[31]*Kirkkonummi – the center of the parish with the same name. It is located about 31km west of Helsinki, next to Espoo.*
[32]*Pakila – a district of Helsinki located about 11km north of the city center.*

So I left the station until I arrived at an intersection and stopped. I called the dispatcher and described the situation. I let them know that we needed another taxi to take a guy to Kirkkonummi.

Three or four minutes later, the other taxi arrived and the Finn got in it and started heading west. Me along with the other gentleman continued going east. The gentleman was so tired of his night that he fell asleep instantly and woke up when we arrived at his house.

I left him there and started driving back towards Tapiola. On the Kehä I, again in Pakila my phone started ringing. It was the calling center. I looked at the phone and thought, what now? "Hi, you had a customer and you ordered him a new taxi which went to Kirkkonummi?" "Yes, I did, is something wrong?" I asked. "The customer says he left his wallet in your car. Is it there?" Kitty asked me. I told her "Hold on, I'll stop the car or else I'll be the one needing to be found, doing 80-90km/h."

I stopped in the first bus stop I saw. I looked around in the car but couldn't see anything out of the ordinary. I told Kitty, "I don't see a wallet. There's nothing unfamiliar in the car." To that, Kitty only said, "Got it. We'll tell him." The conversation ended. I drove to Espoo and ended the night with this adventure. I needed a little rest myself.

I have no idea where the Clown had left his wallet. Maybe he left it at the hotel when he rushed to get on the taxi. Anyway when I got to Espoo, I checked again. I looked everywhere but I didn't found any wallets.

## The unbreakable old man who had fallen off a bridge

A late night in **May**. I was sitting at the taxi stand in **Kilo[33], eastern Espoo**, to take a little break and have a cigarette. I could finish my smoke when a fare popped up on Data – **the Espoo police station.** Great. As it was already dark outside and the order came from the police station, I was beginning to imagine what kind of customer it would be. I was wondering how far could I drive before I need to call the police again.

Because the police station is as big as a shopping center, it wasn't easy to find the right door. I was circling around the building.

---

[33]*Kilo* – *a little district of Espoo. A part of the Suur-Leppävaara area. It is located about 14km northwest of Helsinki.*

I was just turning the car around when I saw a door open from the corner of the building. It was a lanky, tired older man with glasses. He seemed to be well in his 50s. He was wearing a worn down brownish jacket and dirty, shabby jeans. My first thoughts were that this guy couldn't have money and what was he even doing in the station – why was he there or why was he brought there?

He approached the car and I asked him if he had ordered the taxi. It turned out he had. I welcomed him into the car.

Before anything I asked the guy with his crooked, old glasses, if he even has any money. "Yeah, sure I do," the old man told me. I said: "Show me, I don't believe you." "I got it, don't worry," he told me. I repeated myself: "Show me, or we aren't going anywhere." Then the old man showed me a ragged 20-euro bill. So I asked: "Where do you want to go?" "To Espoo, ...tie." Oh great, I know that place. You can find all kinds of folks there.

We started driving to Espoo center. On the way I inquired about what had brought him to the police station where usually people aren't voluntarily. "I fell off a bridge," the man told me. "I'm sorry, WHAT?! How? A bridge? How did you do that?" I had quite a few questions right away. He kindly explained: "I was on the bridge looking at the fishes and went too far off the ledge. I lost my balance and fell down, head-first onto the tarmac..." "Wait, where were the fishes then?" I asked him. I couldn't quite understand the story. "I don't know where they were either. I was too drunk," the guy gave a more logical answer. *Well, aren't you quite the fellow*, I thought. I kept asking: "Didn't you break anything then?" "Oh, no-no, I'm good. I landed like a young cat. I bent my glasses a bit, though," the man gave an unbelievable answer. I glanced at the guy and noticed that his glasses really did get damaged a bit. I still wasn't satisfied, though. I wanted to know more and kept asking: "Where did this happen? Which bridge did you fall off of?" "The one in Espoo center near the church," he explained.

I know the place. The road goes over it and there is a tunnel for pedestrians underneath it. I just don't understand how he saw fishes there... He must have had enough alcohol in him to see fishes in the tarmac...

He was in a good mood though. On the way he hummed to a song by Boney M, ironically called "Rivers of Babylon." I guess he had a reason to be happy

– falling on the tarmac from about 3 meters and getting no injuries. I still couldn't believe it.

We arrived at his house. He paid the bill and asked me where his backpack was. I told him: "You didn't have one. You entered the car, both hands in your pockets." "Oh, okay, I must have left it at the station," he calmly answered.

And like that, he took off. I was wondering for a while how he managed to fall off the bridge like he said he did, and not injure himself. Unbelievable and at the same time a bit comical.

## A woman called the emergency service because her husband wasn't answering his phone

**July.** Early morning on a workday. About 4am I picked up a guy with an injured foot from **Kivenlahti**[34], **Espoo**. He was about 30-35 years old. Sleepy and half-drunk, half hung-over guy who wanted to go to another multi-story house. We had about a kilometer to drive.

During that short time he gave me an overview of where he was coming and what had happened.

---

[34]*Kivenlahti – a district in the southwestern part of Espoo. It is located about 20km west of Helsinki.*

He told me that they had been drinking beer and watching TV in the evening with a friend. There was more beer than necessary, though, and he had fallen asleep in front of the TV. When he left home, though, he had told his wife that he would be back by midnight. That plan didn't work.

At maybe 2-3am, his wife had called him on his phone but neither he nor his friend heard it. They were calmly sleeping their beer-filled dreams. Finally, at 4am the sleep wasn't so deep anymore and after several calls the guy finally woke up to his wife calling.

The wife was so angry, he wasn't sure if he could get into his house. He explained that his wife was also irrationally jealous. She had thought that her husband is somewhere enjoying himself with another woman. Like that wasn't enough, she had called the emergency service and told them that her husband is missing... To that, the guy asked me: "Can you imagine a person with this kind of fantasy, who could do such a thing? I just fell asleep at a friend's house and the broad has me announced missing..." I really didn't know what to say. I just thought to myself, *nobody's asking you to be with such a woman. It's your free will.*

### "Listen to the taxi driver next time!"

**July.** Nighttime on a workday. It was about 3am. Where do you go for adventures if not **Espoo center**[35].

I was sitting on the taxi stand and a guy entered, about 30 years old. I asked where to go. "**Kivenlahti**," was the answer. "Which street exactly?" I inquired. "Yläjuoksu," he told me as I got a more precise location.

I fed the address into the GPS and we started moving. He started calling somewhere. About 200m from the taxi stand there was an intersection, where the navigation system suggested going right. I started to turn right but the guy on the phone, sitting next to me, started waving his hand telling me to go left. I told him: "Actually you get to Kivenlahti if you turn right here and it's the faster way," but the dude started arguing. He just told me, the phone call still going on, "I have been living in Espoo for 35 years and I know which way is faster." I gave up and just said: "It doesn't make a difference for me which way we go. As long as you're happy," and added: "but honestly, I'm not aware of a street called Yläjuoksu in Kivenlah-

---

[35]***Espoo center*** - *a district of Central Espoo. It is located about 22km west of Helsinki.*

ti." "Yes there is, I know there is," the guy kept arguing confidently and continued talking on his phone.

So we were driving towards Kivenlahti. At every intersection, my GPS told me to make a U-turn. I was thinking maybe the GPS wanted me to go through **Kauklahti**[36]. The way I wanted to go when I started to turn right.

We got to **Espoonlahti**, next to Kivenlahti, where the GPS told me to turn towards **Hanko**[37], on the highway. I told the guy that and immediately asked: "Are you completely sure that Yläjuoksu is in Kivenlahti?" I explained: "My GPS shows that there's 24 minutes to go… It seems to be farther than that…" The guy became anxious and decided to check the address.

He called his girlfriend, who he was going to visit. I heard the guy asking: "Hey, what area is the Yläjuoksu-street in? It's in Kivenlahti, right?" I heard the girl answer something after which the guy was astonished and loudly said: "In **NIIPPERI??**"[38] and swore: "For fuck's sake!!"

---

[36]***Kauklahti*** *– a district in the western part of Espoo near Kehä III motorway. It is located about 24km west of Helsinki.*
[37]***Hanko*** *– a bilingual port town and municipality on the south coast of Finland, 130 kilometers west of Helsinki.*
[38]***Niipperi*** *– a district in northern Espoo located about 23km northwest of Helsinki.*

He ended the call. We looked at each other and both started laughing out loud. "In Niipperi, yeah-yeah, I have been living here for 35 years," I ironically repeated his confident wisdom. He admitted: "Yeah, you were right, you were right. I should have listened to you and turned right at the first intersection and followed the GPS." He continued: "Of course it's in Niipperi not in damn Kivenlahti!"

I think he had used some kind of substance because he was talking to himself. And the next moment, he was talking to me again. During the trip I had to ask him several times: "Did you say something to me?" to which he just answered "Oh, no, I was just thinking out loud." He looked kind of Rastafarian. It wouldn't surprise me if he had previously smoked a certain plant that had influenced his orientating skills.

Anyway, we finally arrived at the right address and he saw his girlfriend who was already waiting on the street.

Later, when I checked the GPS for my own interest to see how far the destination was from Espoo center, and it turned out that the trip we made was about 16km longer.

### From a sauna to a night club with a Singaporean

**April. Tapiola, southeast Espoo.** I picked up a Singaporean businessman from a private house at midnight on a weekend. He was visiting his Finnish friend and had just left the sauna. His face was still glowing and even his hair was wet. They were probably sipping some beer in the sauna – the gentleman was in a pleasantly tipsy state.

At first he wanted to go to a nearby hotel, but then a friend called him, who invited him to a nightclub in **Helsinki**. During his phone call, I asked him which nightclub the friend was at, where should we drive to. The foreigner, being tipsy, told me the name but I couldn't understand him. I asked again and he gave a different answer every time. It was like we were playing a game of telephone – his friend told him the name of the club and he tried to repeat it to me. It was no use, though.

I told him to ask the address of the club. That didn't work either because the Singaporean didn't hear what the Finn said. He was inside the club, in the middle of all the action, trying to give us information. Instead of going to a place more quiet and telling us the name then, he was still trying to give us the name of the club to a drunk foreigner in the middle of the noise.

Finally I offered the Singaporean that the Finn could tell me the name and address instead of telling him. He gave me his phone. Through all the loud noise the Finn tried to give me the name and address. I still didn't exactly understand what the name was and where it was. I just got a hunch what the name could be.

I called the information line, offering the operator a variety of names. They told me that they don't know any clubs by those names. **Calle, Galle** or whatever the fuck it was. The operator was trying to find a club by that name in the database, but it was no use. I didn't know any clubs by that name either.

I finally got the street and the number of the house from the Finn. But he told me the wrong number. I think he said 12, it was really 40. We set a course for Helsinki.

I was in Tapiola, just turning towards Helsinki on one of the main streets, when the Singaporean thought it would be a good idea to take a piss. He asked me if there were any fuel stations nearby. I looked to the right, at a dark spot next to a fence and told him: "You can do your thing right here, there isn't anyone looking.

You can even go under the trees." He thought for a bit but couldn't hold it anymore. Better to feel a bit of shame than piss your pants. I stopped the car and he went and did his business. When he was ready, we continued towards Helsinki in a relieved mood.

On the way he started to doubt his plan, though. He said: "Damn, I so tired, I shouldn't go. Maybe I should go to sleep in my hotel." I offered him: "You can always change your mind, if you want to," to which he told me: "Nah, I can't. I promised my friend I would go," and continued to convince himself: "Sleeping is for the weak. When I get to Singapore, I'll have plenty of time to do that." He became ecstatic: "Damn, that Finnish sauna was good. I didn't want to leave! When I get home, I'm going to have one built for myself. It's just that great!"

So I drove the friendly Singaporean to Kasarmikatu street, Helsinki. We started looking for building number 12, as the Finn told us. We couldn't find it. We were swearing together with the foreigner. Now the idea to go sleep in the hotel seemed pretty good, because we couldn't even find his friend and the club. We thought maybe he had told us the wrong street too, not just the number. We decided to find out.

I noticed three gentlemen standing on the sidewalk and discussing something. I stopped the car next to them and asked if they know a nightclub called "kalle", "galle" or "karla." "Oh, yeah-yeah, Galle is near here! Keep driving on this street and you'll soon see it," the Finnish gentlemen kindly guided us while laughing at the names I suggested.

In about 400 meters we arrived at the club. Even then the Singaporean doubted if he should go into the club being so tired. I offered again: "You can still go back, you have a chance. I can take you back to Espoo." He still decided to go in, as he promised his friend.

The man paid the bill, shook my hand and exited the car, leaving me with a half a can of warm beer instead of a tip.


### "Damn it! My 7-year-old shoes brought from Spain have just been stolen!"

**July.** Early morning. The sun was already up. There was an order about 500 meters from the taxi stand in **Tapiola, southeast Espoo.** I picked up a tipsy gentleman in his 30s.

He was wearing a t-shirt and shorts. When he sat next to me, I noticed that he wasn't wearing any shoes.

I asked him: "Weren't you wearing anything on your feet? Were you barefoot or are your shoes around here somewhere?" I turned out that they weren't. He explained that he had taken a nap in the bus stop because he wanted to rest for A BIT. But the rest had gotten a little long. When he woke up 1.5 hours later, he noticed that someone had stolen his old Italian shoes. He complained: "Damn it! I brought them from Spain myself 7 years ago. I don't understand who needed my sweaty and stretched out shoes."

He wasn't sad about the theft, though. He was rather disturbed about the fact that the shoes had lasted for 7 years and were brought from Spain.

I asked him where he would like to go. His first wish was: "Let's go to the Shell in **Suomenoja**[39] (about 7km) to buy a lighter – I really need a smoke."

We drove to the Shell. When he had his cigarette, we kept moving to **Siuntio**[40] (about 30km) county.

On the way he told me, among other things, how speed cameras work and the speeds you can be driving with without getting a ticket.

---

[39]*Suomenoja* – *in the southern part of Espoo in the district of Kaitaa. It is located about 14km west of Helsinki.*
[40]*Siuntio* – *a parish in Finland located about 45km west of Helsinki.*

Considering it was early morning, he had a sharper mind than mine after a 12-hour shift. I had a tough time keeping up with the intelligent topics. It seemed like the hard partying had no effect on him. But dealing with people in this condition had taken its toll on me.

*4. Our early morning "product" of "creativity."*

I took the barefooted man home and finished my adventures. The time was 8:30am. I had driven a couple hundred kilometers and been behind the wheel for 13 hours. When I put the car to "bed," I met my Finnish friend Richard. We made a chair while having a few long drinks. You see what we can generate after these kind of rounds.

## ARROGANT OR JUST STUPID?

Everything isn't always funny and comical in Finland. Unfortunately unpleasant arrogance and annoying stupidity aren't rare here. I tried to make this chapter as short as I could, but sadly there are too many stories about these kinds of people. Stories about people who make you wonder if they are arrogant or just stupid. You can be the judge of that.

### What's wrong with you that you are so blatantly cocky?

**October**. Two slightly tipsy boneheads walked to the taxi stand in **Matinkylä, southern Espoo** – a woman and a man who I think was her son. It was about 6pm. They wanted to go to an apartment building in **Leppävaara** district in **eastern Espoo**, on the border of **Helsinki** and **Espoo**.

I drove to the destination quickly and without any problems. When we arrived, I asked which house was theirs, so I would know where to stop. The answer to my inquiry was snippy: "We have no idea! You have to know which house is the right one!" I have to know? Some people have a strange understanding. I have to know where you live and where you want to exit the car? So I independently made a turn towards an apartment building. To that they started yelling smugly: "Stop the meter now!!!"

The couple thought they were joking, laughing about the "comedy" that had just happened.

I stopped the meter and calmly answered: "See, I stopped it. You don't have to yell." For the trip, the woman offered me 20 euros "under the table." I answered emphatically: "NO WAY! You will pay according to the meter like you have to!" I don't understand what some people think of themselves – they come in the taxi, yelling, mocking, being cocky and then they offer to pay the bill underhand. Makes you wonder what is wrong with some people who act like that.

### Espoonlahti's egomaniac

End of **May**. Afternoon. I was sitting at the stand in **Espoonlahti, southwest Espoo.** I was waiting for a preordered fare that was supposed to go to **Helsinki-Vantaa International Airport**[41] in **Vantaa** (about

---

[41]*Helsinki-Vantaa airport – the biggest airport in Finland, about 500 flights depart every day, 15 million people go through the air-*

35km). A nice long stint meant about 60 euros extra in the till.

I finally got my fare. It had been ordered only 100m away from the taxi stand, to an apartment building. I drove there, parked the car next to the doorway and was ready to leave whenever the client arrived.

When the time shown in the order was up, I began to call the client to ask if and when he would be coming. I called seven times, but the line was constantly busy. I finally went in front of the doorway. I tried to see where he lived from the residents' list. I found the name and the apartment number, so I called him from the door. Again, nobody answered. I tried three times.

I thought, okay – another bullshit fare and got in the car. I was just marking the fare void when a cocky dumbbell, about 30 years old, exited the doorway with a pink suitcase and the phone next to his ear.

I put his pink piggy into the boot and we sat in the car. Between his babbling, the imbecile managed to tell me: "To the airport." Like I wasn't aware where the dumbbell wanted to go – the order had all the info. So I asked the "VIP": "Which terminal are you heading to – 1

---

*port every year. It is located 18 kilometers north of the city center of Helsinki.*

or 2?" Again, a short answer was all he managed: **"Finnair**[42]**."** He couldn't even fucking say the number of the terminal, he just had to say the company. Fortunately I knew that Finnair flights depart from the terminal 2.

We managed to drive about a hundred meters when the fucker decided to take the floor: "Hey, turn off the radio. I can't hear anything on the phone." My radio was playing so quietly, it could barely be heard. I was furious. What a complete fucking ape. I turned the radio off and drove to the airport with his babbling accompanying me... Definitely better than anything on the radio. Definitely.

What a guy. Orders a taxi, doesn't come out at the right time, doesn't answer his phone or the door. No "hello," no "please," no "thank you" – only constant whining and moaning. Where do these people come from, I ask.

---

[42]*__Finnair Plc__ (Finnish: Finnair Oyj, Swedish: Finnair Abp) is the flag carrier and largest airline of Finland, with its headquarters in Vantaa and its main hub at Helsinki-Vantaa Airport. Finnair and its subsidiaries dominate both domestic and international air travel in Finland. Its major shareholder is the government of Finland.*

### The orientating skills of women should be investigated

**April**. I drove a client to a bar in **Helsinki** and a guy waved me down in front of the same bar: "Hey, could you pick up a girl?" I looked at the young lady and evaluated her in my mind: "Ooh, that's a pretty decent bird, of course I'll pick her up." Well, it was far from a chick, when she finally managed to approach the car and landed on the back seat. It turned out to be a wasted woman, in her forties, who had the best opinion of herself. She instantly started testing my nerves.

At the start of the drive I asked her for the address of the destination. I didn't get it. So I asked again: "Where should I go if you won't tell me the address?" "Just keep driving," the woman probably on her period told me. I stopped the car to the arrogant attitude and told her resolutely: "I'm not driving anywhere until I get an address." She then gave me the wrong address as it turned out. Throughout the whole drive she complained and whined at me as well as some invisible characters. She didn't seem quite right in the head.

We arrived at the address she gave me and she started complaining that I brought her to the wrong address. At first I calmly told her: "You're the one who gave me the address." She kept saying she gave me a different one and kept on arguing and insulting me. So I took her 300 meters to the other side of the building according to her directions where it suited her to stop and pay the bill. Then she started whining that I didn't know where she lived. To that I told her pretty angrily: "Please, pay the damn bill and get lost! Next time give me the right address then you can get to the right place, you drunk moron!" She paid the bill, exited the car and closed the door with force, still complaining about something outside.

I backed up and exited the yard and left to have a cigarette in a nearby parking lot. You can't do your job if a moron has just screwed your nerves up. Then you're going to pick up the next client and insult him. You can only do this job well if you're relaxed and in a good mood yourself.

Oh well, a weekend just like any other. You will be so full of these "adventures" in the morning that a single beer will be enough. Actually you don't even need a beer after finishing your round. If you drive around with drunk, yelling, screaming, complaining people for 12-14 hours, you'll be completely hammered in the morning. You'd just like to tell these people: "Damn it, try to be a decent human being, the taxi driver is also human!" The simpleminded apes don't understand that when they use a taxi for 10, 20 or 30 minutes and keep complaining and screaming, then they might think it's a one-time thing. The driver has to deal with that shit for 12 hours. And almost every night.

## The Kerava clowns
End of **January**. I had landed in **Kerava** with some young people from the city center of **Helsinki** at about 4am. It's a small town with about 35000 inhabitants, about 31km north of Helsinki. The Sinebrychoff beer factory, which makes the world famous Koff beer, is also here.

But back to the round. I had just left the youngsters from Helsinki when I got a fare from the local McDonald's. I found the diner but not the client. There were about 15-20 people near the McDonald's, but none of them approached my car.

About 30 meters away from the diner, a slick guy about 20-22 years old, was walking to my car.

He started to talk to me like we knew each other: "Hey, give us a ride!" Without any emotion, I responded: "I can't. I'm not allowed to pick up a client if you haven't ordered a taxi." Just in case, I asked him: "Did you order this taxi?" "Yes!" was the answer, clearly a lie. I then asked: "What's the order number?" "Uhm, but that isn't important," he said, trying to talk me into it. I told him: "Yes, it is," and asked for the number again. The smooth guy told me that he didn't remember. At the same time he tried to enter the car, pulling the rear door. But I had locked the doors. To avoid any "surprises," I always lock the doors from the inside when driving to an unfamiliar place during the night. I lock them even in Helsinki, when driving through the crowds in the city center. I have several experiences where people try to enter the car while I'm on the move.

He was surprised: "Damn it, are your doors locked? Open them!" I laughed and told him: "No I won't, you haven't ordered this taxi." Slick started talking me into it again: "Well I haven't, but come on, take us, I'll give you 20 euros." I told him: "I don't want your money. Maybe the client who ordered the taxi is still coming." He wasn't satisfied and was still going on: "Come on, I don't think the client is coming. Give us a ride! Look, my girl is right here and well, we need to go home to get it on." Like I give I damn, if you're banging that chick, I thought. I told him again: "I will not pick you up. I'm waiting for my customer."

*5. Behind the Sinebrychoff factory in Kerava, next to Lahdenväylä, there is a commercial Koff can, a few meters high.*

At the same time a police bus appeared from behind the corner. They were probably just making their routine check because the outside of the McDonald's seemed to be the most active place in Kerava. The guy ignored the police and kept on haggling. The cops thought the conversation between us seemed suspicious. The policemen approached the car to ask if everything was in order. I told them: "Yes, everything is fine, we're just having a conversation." Hearing that, they left.

I looked around and didn't see my client anywhere so I thought what the heck, I'll pick up Mister

Slick. Better to get some money than to just drive back to Helsinki with an empty car.

So I asked the clown where they were going, what was the address. He told me he would direct me where to go. I told him: "Okay, good."

Slick and his chick sat in the back. Suddenly some bonehead opened the passenger door and entered the car, pretty hammered. I looked at the horny couple in the back and asked: "Is this your friend?" "Yeah-yeah, he's with us, he's driving too," Slick told me.

I turned to the street from the McDonald's. We drove a few hundred meters, arriving at a crossroads. Suddenly someone from the back says: "Turn right!" And then another direction: "No, left," then another order: "Turn around!" "What the hell?" I asked to that kind of bullshit. I asked: "Where do I go then? Right, left or do I turn around?" "No-no, turn around," Slick told me. I was cursing to myself that there's always trouble when you let some drunk idiots guide you.

So I turned around and we were headed the way Slick had told me. Suddenly the chick in the back started complaining: "Why are we driving so far?" Slick explained her: "We're taking our friend home first and then we'll return." The girl didn't agree and told me: "No-no-no, that's enough, stop right here! We're leaving. We live right here."

I pulled over. Okay, for fuck's sake, just go. It's better to deal with one clown that with three. The meter was showing exactly 10 euros for the distance driven. So we had driven about 660 meters. I asked them: "Who is paying the bill?" to which the chick said that they want to split the bill. What the fuck – 10 euros and a split. I asked: "Are you bored and you have nothing else to do, so you drive for 10euros and then want to split it?" I was of course cursing myself that there's no damn need to pick up clowns like these.

So I split the bill. The girl paid 5 euros of the 10 euro bill, BY CARD... At the same time, Slick had exited the car and left the rear street-side door open. He was standing on the street with hands in his pockets. That caught the attention of the patrolling police again. Again, they approached us and asked: "Everything in order?" I told them yes again and started to drive with the last clown left in the car.

Right when we got going he started asking: "How much is the meter showing?" I told him: "5.70. Don't worry, your pal paid half the bill for you." "Oh, okay," the clown calmed down.

We arrived at his house and he paid the "enormous" 8.80 euro bill. During his payment, he looked like he was being ordered to pay a million dollars for the circus that had happened.

### A hyperactive ignorant brainless chicken

On an evening in **January** at about 10pm I got a fare in **Haukilahti, southern Espoo**, next to **Westend**. It was a private house.

I drove there and two people entered the car. A guy, about 40 years old and a lady about 10 years younger.Both pleasantly tipsy. One chick stayed outside. I asked the couple sitting in the car where we were going. "Not far. To Kuutamo bar in **Olari** (about 3km)," the guy answered.

Okay. I entered the address to the navigator and waited for the chick left outside to enter the car so we could go. She was calmly smoking a cigarette though. Then she suddenly thought it was a good idea to start cleaning out snow from the yard. She took a shovel off the wall and started to clean off the snow next to the car.

Finally when I had waited for her for a few minutes I asked through the car window: "Are you coming today?" She put the shovel down and got in the car. She sat in the front and right away started touching the buttons on the radio. She found the volume button and turned the volume up. She turned it to a level that hurt my ears. I tolerated it. I didn't say anything, I just secretly turned the volume down using the buttons on the steering wheel. After some time she noticed it and turned it up again. I still didn't say anything. I turned it down a bit again.

Then the Chicken thought that she must groom her feathers. Of course she couldn't do it at home because she had to shovel snow.

The hen was trying to make herself pretty and started to paint her lips. Of course she needed a mirror to do that. She pulled down the sun shade so hard that it hit the rear view mirror and pushed it crooked towards the ceiling. I quietly observed what she did and still said nothing. I thought to myself, should I say something or would it be no use to educate an imbecile during the last two minutes of the drive. I decided to be quiet. I guess the Chicken noticed my tight face muscles and asked me with the most innocent face: "Everything OK?" I looked at her with a face that said, "What do you think?" and ironically told her: "Yes, everything is great!" That ended our conversation.

What else can you say to a brainless bird like that? She wouldn't understand you anyway.

I took them to the bar, the Chicken paid the bill and everyone left the car like nothing had happened at all.


### The screaming German in Helsinki
**September**. This happened at about 4.30am in **Helsinki**. I was just returning from **East-Helsinki** where I had just taken a client. The direction was back towards the city center.

I had just turned down to a smaller street from **Itäväylä**[43], when two guys in their twenties waved at me from the right side of the road. I stopped the car, presuming the men wanted to go somewhere. They turned out to be two drunken Germans who needed to go to a hotel called Rantaspi, Rantapi or Rantansity in **Vantaa**. Try to understand Germans trying to pronounce a Finnish name in English while they're drunk. When I later looked for the hotel on the Internet, I realized it was the **Rantasipi** hotel next to the **Helsinki-Vantaa airport**.

---

[43]*Itäväylä – a multilane highway from Helsinki towards east to Itäsalmi district, about 20 km long.*

I asked them several times: what is the name of the hotel? I couldn't understand shit. I asked if they knew the address or if they had anything with the hotel's name or address. Nothing.

Then the guys asked me if I knew any Citymarkets or K-Markets near the hotel. Well, I hadn't seen any near the airport, because there are only about two specific routes I take when I go there. On those roads I have only seen a big Jumbo shopping center.

So I told them I wasn't aware of a Citymarket next to the airport, which boggled their minds. They asked me how the hell could I not know such a thing, "being a taxi driver and all." I wanted to ask them if they know the burger shot next to the big building in Frankfurt. Oh you don't? What the fuck guys?!

One of the guys sat in the front during the conversation. But when he saw that I didn't know where they needed to go, he got out of the car and slammed the door behind him. Like that wasn't enough, he yelled to me: "Haah, fuck you, fuck you!" moving away and towards the car and looking pissed. What a jackass.

The other dude was sitting in the back. We tried to solve the problem. We spoke calmly. I explained to him that I hadn't heard of a hotel by that name, never

ever. He called his pissed-off buddy back to the car and apologized to me, but his friend wouldn't listen. He was still screaming while walking back and forth on the autumnal Finnish grass.

I told the calm guy sitting in the car that I could call the information line and ask about the hotel and where it could be. That it wouldn't be a problem. But his friend kept yelling, swinging his fists at me and at some invisible people while still screaming "Fuck you, fuck you!" I was starting to get irritated myself. I wanted to get out of the car and take out my frustration. But why should I ruin my shift for an imbecile?

I finally told the calm guy in the backseat: "Please leave my car. I am not taking you anywhere. Your friend is acting very aggressively and I don't need any problems." He didn't argue and exited the car right away. I started to drive away, the passenger side window open. The yelling idiot jogged next to the car and was still cursing. "Fuck you, fuck you!!" I had had enough and yelled back: "Fuck you too, you fucking moron!" Hearing that, the German started boiling, screaming even louder and trying to kick the car. I pulled away from him a bit, when I saw him trying to do that. When I saw he was planning to really damage it, I just drove away. I watched him receding in the mirror, still trying to catch up ...

## The "intelligent" conversations with the bone-headed inhabitants of the woods

**September**. The weekend. At about 3 am I ended up in **Järvenperä** district in the northern part of **Espoo** after taking some clients there from **Espoo center.** I thought that was it, I'll be venturing in this forest forever. Usually that's how it is – when you end up in the bushes you keep going deeper into the wilderness. That's how it was for a while.

I got a fare that took me even deeper into the woods. So deep that the pavement ended and became a dirt road. That is rare in **Espoo**.

After wondering around the roads for about 10 minutes, I arrived at the right place. I drove into a dark yard. I could see some farmhouse lights about 25 meters away. There were three guys standing in the yard, two of them approached the car right away and got in – their booking number matched the one on Data. Then a bald guy sipping beer approached the driver side window and asked: "What's the number of the order?" I smirked and said: "I can't tell you. You are the client, you have to tell me." Baldy wasn't the sharpest tool in the box and asked again: "What's the number of the order?" By now I was laughing, and answered: "Well, what's the number then?" Baldy got angry, raising his voice and asked now with an insistent irritated tone: "I have to tell you?" He got even angrier and maliciously asked: "What's the damn order number?" I didn't get a chance to answer him as the guy sitting next to me solved the situation: "Zero five is the number. It's our taxi!" "Okay, okay, whatever," the Baldy shot back and walked back to the fence surrounding the yard with his beer. He kept staring at me with an angry face like he was saying: "If I ever see you again, I'll crush you like the beer can in my hand." I laughed as I looked at him and we began our trip with the other guys.

Fuck me, then I started another "intelligent" and "friendly" conversation with the next guy. I asked them: "Where are you headed?" The guy next to me: "To **Kaisankoti**[44]." I asked: "Do you know the address?" "Don't you?" the guy responded. I told him that I didn't, that I couldn't memorize every address. The dummy asked: "Are you new?" I told him: "No I'm

---

[44]*Kaisankoti – a health center in thenorth part of Espoo, about 30km northwest of Helsinki.*

not. It doesn't matter if I'm old or new, you can't memorize every place." Damn dumbass, I have to remember every bar, school and company and now some random *koti* also? Like I haven't anything else in my life to remember. He kept on going: "Well yeah, but its Kaisankoti, you should know that anyway." I didn't want to keep arguing and kept it short: "Well I don't!"

Actually we were told about the place in taxi school and I think it was even in the exam but if you don't go there, you won't remember it.

Anyway that topic ended and we continued on some more important matters. Among other things we talked about the Russians. He said that there were too many of them in the area. They caused problems with robberies and stealing. He explained that earlier people left their doors unlocked when they left. When the Russians came, nobody could do that anymore. He also said that the immigrant Slavs didn't want to work.

It sounded logical, if their only work was robbing and stealing. On the other hand the Russians were sucking every euro they could from Finland by requesting financial aid. They were a pretty big headache in the area. He didn't say anything bad about

Estonians though – Estonians go to Finland to get a job and to be helpful. They have a reputation as hard-working, paying their taxes, etc. "Well, good to hear," I thanked him for the kind words. I don't know if he meant it or was just being polite because he was speaking to an Estonian himself. But I have heard the same thing from other Finns.

### "Fuck you!" "Fuck you too!"

On an early morning in **June** at about 3.30 am I got a fare in **Kivenlahti**, **southwest Espoo** to a popular kiosk pub called Casanova.

I drove to the pub. There were a couple dozen people outside. First an old lady raised her arm, she was away from the crowd. I stopped the car. She got in the car right away, without telling me the order number. I asked for the number and she said 97. The right number was actually 37.

Oh well, I thought. I'll let her stay in the car and turned on the meter to take the old woman home.

When passing the crowd I saw an older gentle-man and a younger guy on the street. They stopped me and asked if the taxi was available. I told them that I wasn't anymore. They got irritated and told me that they had ordered the taxi and they should be in it. I told them: "Sorry, but I'm not vacant anymore," and kept driving. The window was open so I heard how one of them yelled at me angrily: "Fuck you!" I responded with: "Fuck you too!" You can curse all you want, but I'm the one driving away and you are the one left behind on the street.

### The biker, the pointless guy and the drunk cow
A Sunday evening in **September**. I got my first fare of the shift next to **Kivenlahti**, in **Espoonlahti** from a pub.

A woman about 40 years old got in, clearly drunk. She told me: "To Zardrinkadu." "Excuse me, what was that?" I asked politely. "Hezerdringadu," was the similar answer. Fuck, I couldn't understand what the hell she was mumbling. "Where-where-where," I asked again. Then I understood that the drunk cow wants to go to Fredrikrinkatu street in **Helsinki** (about 16km).

I started driving and the hag suddenly yelled: "Wait, more people are coming." And they did. Two people entered the car. A guy and a girl about 25-30 years old and a biker about 40-45 years old. Everyone was completely hammered.

As said, the destination was in Helsinki, so I turned towards Helsinki in Espoonlahti. The biker didn't like that idea. He wanted to go to Kivenlahti, which was the other way. I stopped the car on the side of the road and asked them to decide who was going where.

The biker won and we started to go towards Kivenlahti. Right away he started to give out commands: "Put some music on!" I saw that he didn't have his seatbelt on so I responded with: "Put your seatbelt on!" "Put some music on," the biker repeated himself. I also repeated my request: "Put your seatbelt on!" He didn't want to comply and kept asking for music. I told him: "I will put some music on when you put your seatbelt on." The younger guy in the back agreed with me and also told the biker to put on his seatbelt. The biker got a little angry and told me: "Don't fuck with me!" I told him: "I'm not. You're fucking with me by not wanting to put on your seatbelt." I added: "These aren't my rules. You have to put on your seatbelt."So, dripping sweat and alcohol, he put on his seatbelt for the last 200m. We had almost gotten to his house during the argument.

The bonehead exited and I headed to Helsinki. The two youngsters in the back started arguing loudly on the highway. They got in some kind of a fight. The cow in the backseat thought it was a good time to take off her shoe. She took it off and hit his leg against my elbow. When she got her shoe off, she kept squirming around like she had ants in her pants. The voices got louder in the back again, adding to the squirming. The noise disturbed the cow and she threatened to throw them both out if they didn't calm down. The younger woman promised to throw out the older woman. They went back and forth for about a minute and then calmed down.

After about 15 minutes of circus we arrived in Helsinki. On Pohjois-Rautatiekatu street, with about 300 meters to go until the destination, the younger lady started yelling. He had a problem with me turning onto another street instead of going straight. The older cow then explained that you couldn't even go straight because a one-way street ended there. "What do you mean you can't?" She kept yelling and added confidently: "Sure you can!"

I didn't say anything the whole trip because I was just too lazy to interfere. I had nothing to say anyway. I could have thrown them out or drive them to the destination. If I had started arguing, there would have just been another idiotic yeller.

The younger cow definitely needed cooling down. She needed to be thrown in cold water. She was the one who yelled and complained the most. Uncontrollably and arrogantly.

A "calm" Sunday night in Finland.


### Clients who don't know where they're going
**October**. I picked up two businessmen, about 40 years old, in **Viherlaakso**[45]**, eastern Espoo** in the morning. We had to pick up another guy in **Pitäjänmäki**[46], northwest part of **Helsinki**, before going to **Vantaa** airport. Right at the beginning of the drive I asked where the third gentleman lived. "In Pitäjänmäki," was the answer. "Where exactly in Pitäjänmäki do I have to go?" I asked. "Wait, let me check," one of the gentlemen answered.

What the hell? You're sitting at home the whole evening before. Couldn't you have found time to call him and ask for his address? I thought to myself. You could find out where you need to go in the morning.

---

[45]***Viherlaakso*** - *a district of East-Espoo. It is located about 20km in north-west of Helsinki.*

[46]***Pitäjänmäki*** *– a district in northwest Helsinki, about 9 kilometers from the city center.*

But no, you get in the taxi and you have no idea where to go.

We arrived at the destination. There were three apartment buildings all with the same number but different doorway letters. I asked the guy who gave me the address which one was the house of the third gentleman. I would have driven closer to the house and the right doorway so it would be more convenient for the guy probably coming with a suitcase. He gave me the number of the house. I told him "I know the number, but all three of the houses have the same number. Which one of these is your friend coming out of?" He answered with: "I don't know." Finally I saw someone approaching from the right with a suitcase from the corner of my eye. It was the right gentleman.

So we drove to the airport. Right before arriving I asked the "wise" guy again: "Which terminal are you going to, where does the flight depart?" He didn't know.

Unbelievable! You are going on a trip and you don't know shit! Are you an imbecile? I then told him: "I don't remember which terminal this company has either. Check the ticket, it must be on there!" Then he finally checked and confirmed that it was the first terminal. "Thank you very much!" Was that so hard?

### The taxi isn't a dance floor

**October**. I picked up two guys, about 22-23 years old from the **Olari** taxi stand in **southern Espoo**. They wanted to go to a nearby district of private houses, **Eestintaival** (about 3-4km). Right when they got in the car they started demanding: "Turn the radio up a bit!" I turned the volume up. "Louder," they still weren't happy with the volume. "More, a bit more," the brainless guys still weren't satisfied. I had had it and turned the volume up to the maximum, to make their ears hurt just like mine did. Then they were finally happy, sitting with their satisfied faces in the back.

I just don't know what to say, what is going on in some Finnish youngsters' heads. Do they think it's funny to act like that? Or maybe they just want to feel important once or twice a week and they pick the taxi for that.

### Ignorant old lady with disabilities – moving and thinking

**November**. Evening on a regular workday. I got a fare in **Tapiola**, **southeast Espoo** to the underground parking lot of the local Stockmann mall. I have to say, the person who designed the parking house was drunk or overworked. The problem is with entering and exiting the parking house. The gates, which have a barrier in front of them, have so little room between them that you can barely go through with a midsized car. I don't know how people with SUVs manage. And the Hyundai i40 isn't a small car. I'm not complaining just for the fun of it. The metal posts have been scraped and bent with cars. There are clear signs that the gates are too narrow. You have to be an expert driver to be able to get through them.

Anyway, I made my way through without damaging anything. I got into the parking lot and found the client. An older woman, heavy-set, about 60 years old, was waiting for me. She was sitting on a bench with her push-cart.

I jumped out of the car, ecstatic to help the lady. I said hello. No answer from the bench. She started moving her fat ass only after I had opened the front door and moved the seat back. All for her to feel more comfortable and have more room.

Observing the procedure, the Madonna finally got up and pushed herself to the car with the cart. Then she stood with her back to the car, next to the passenger door. I politely told her: "I would take the cart, if I may, and put in the boot. You can sit in the car." The hag asked in an arrogant tone in English: "What?" I calmly explained to her again: "I would take the cart and put it in the back..." Then she understood and answered: "Oh, okay," as she sank into the car.

I lifted the old woman's cart and two plastic bags into the trunk. I wanted to get in myself but then I noticed that Big Mama hadn't even bothered to close the door herself. I closed it for her.

Half of the old women with push-carts for support (well, old women in general) can walk without support but are just simulating being sick so that someone would "service" them. I don't know, maybe they feel more important then...

So I asked Big Mama where we were headed. Right away she started acting out: "Where-where, to ....tie." From the 15,000 streets, I wasn't sure where THIS exact street was. I was hoping I would get some more tips from the lady and asked: "Where would that be?" Of course she told me nothing: "In Tapiola." That's where we were. I told her: "Yes, I understand that it's in Tapiola. What direction is it in, when we exit the parking house?" Then she gave me some more specific directions and we started heading the right way.

We arrived at the woman's doorway, where the theatre continued. I took off her seatbelt, lifted her cart out of the car and put her plastic bags on the cart's handles. Then I opened the car door for her, pushed the cart in front of her so that she could grab onto it when exiting the car and "drive" to her doorway. But she was so fucking ignorant, she wouldn't even open the door for herself. I had to do it. Then she couldn't get up on the first try. I helped her up by pulling her. The whole thing took about 5-6 minutes, which means 4 euros on the meter. Of course I didn't get that because I had stopped the meter for her to pay the bill before she left. The only one to blame was me – I could have added a little extra to the bill by marking **"assisting fee**[47]**"** on the meter. As she was paying with a city card, the city of Espoo would have paid for it. But I forgot because of the short drive.

Anyway, she wasn't happy about me putting the bags on her cart's handles. So I lifted them off the cart. She then asked me to bring them to the doorway. Oh well, what else could I have done. I wanted

---

[47]*Assisting fee - extra tax for helping the client. You can add it to the bill in the meter. It is used when the client's heavy belongings are lifted into the car or the customer is helped in other ways before the drive.*

to, but I couldn't tell her to fuck off. She could call the calling center and complain about the service and who needs that. I lifted the bags in front of her door. She then wiggled to the door with her cart and asked if I could help her open the door. I did. Here you go! Finally I heard the phrase "Thank you!" Then I noticed her accent. I don't think she was a pure Finn, she was Slavic...

### The "Aces" with the broken beer cartons
**November**. Weekend. At about 3-4am I got a fare in **Soukka**, next to **Espoonlahti** in **southwest Espoo**.

I arrived at a parking lot of an apartment building, where there were two guys waiting for me, both about 25 years old. One was a blond queer with tiny eyes, holding a carton of beer. He got into the car next to me, the other queer stayed in the parking lot. The imbecile in the car started talking: "Let's get some cash from an ATM." "Well, okay. Should we go to the nearby K-Market?" I asked in response. "Yes. Let's go there, are you okay with that," the moron asked. I answered: "Yes, of course I am." Just in case, I added: "But if you want to, you can pay by card also." "No-no, I want to see my balance, are you okay with that," the queer asked me, looking at me arrogantly. I was beginning to think that the guy wanted to pick a fight with me.

The K-Market was located on the roof of a parking house. I drove there and the queer started giving out orders: "Wait, leave the car here! Don't drive to the ATM, you okay with that?"

So I stopped about 10 meters from the building and the imbecile went to the ATM. Sitting in the car, I suddenly smelled beer. Where the hell was that coming from? I turned on the lights and lifted the carton of beer up from in front of the passenger seat. I saw that the damn box was leaking – the whole floor was under a sea of beer.

I had had enough. I jumped out of the car, took the wet carton of beer, the queer's dirty backpack and put them on the ground next to the car. I closed the door and yelled to the imbecile: "Fucking idiot! Why the fuck do you come into my car with a broken carton?" I drove off. The queer looked around the corner, yelled back at me and looked where I was going. I was leaving. Keep on walking with your carton of beer at 4am on a winter morning when it's -10 degrees Celsius outside.

I drove away from the parking house and stopped the car again. I took out the wet and stinking floor mat out of the car and tried to slide it against the grass to clean it even a little bit. It didn't really work. I threw it back in the car and drove towards **Matinkylä** district in **southern Espoo**. On the way I picked up a couple idiots of the same kind.

On the way to Matinkylä, I got a fare from the **Niittykumppu** district, between **Olari** and **Tapiola**, to a burger joint. Again, two guys with a carton of beer. My memory was as short as a fly's and I didn't ask if the carton was undamaged. The guys loudly entered the car and wanted to go to Matinkylä.

I drove to their house on the sidewalk between some posts where it was really forbidden to go. To the maneuver on of the jerks commented: "See, the guy knows how to drive! We should leave a tip for that." He had a big mouth but he didn't leave a tip at all. When we arrived at their house they started arguing who should pay the bill. One of the imbeciles paid the bill.

When they had gotten out of the car, I noticed the wet floor mat behind the passenger seat – for fuck's sake, another carton of beer had been broken. I was swearing to myself: "Damn idiots, I don't understand what you're doing with the cartons. Are you smashing them on each other's heads, you morons?"

### The youngsters without brains

**December**. Weekend. I got a fare at night to some row houses in **Leppävaara, eastern Espoo**. The number of the house was …D. The order said that I should wait for the clients in the parking lot.

I drove to the address. There was nobody waiting in the parking lot. After 5-6 minutes, they should be outside, but no. There were 4-5 houses sitting like in a boy scout camp.

I looked for the right number in the dark and found the house lettered C but not D. I called the client and wanted to tell them that I had arrived. I added that I was waiting for them near the C-building and asked where D was so I could drive to the right house.

A tipsy girl answered my call and told me: "Wait, we'll come out right away, we'll meet you halfway." "Okay, thanks," I answered. I waited for a couple of minutes but didn't see anybody moving. I thought I'd look for the right house myself. Who knew, they might have been waiting for me there.

I drove slowly on the sidewalk through a yard and arriving on another sidewalk. I saw that about 70 meters away there were some people walking. I drove to them and the girls said, "Ooh, the taxi is already here!" A young wise guy took the floor: "Hey, you were supposed to wait in the parking lot! Why did you drive here?" I ironically asked: "Is this the parking lot that you're walking here?" He answered: "Well we're still going." I was a bit annoyed already: "Listen, I've been waiting for over 10 minutes looking for you. Do you want the taxi or not?" "Yes, yes, we do," the guy apologized. "Well maybe someone will sit in the car and we could go," I offered.

There were 9 of them though – 4 girls and 5 young jerks. They had ordered two taxis but I didn't see the other one. It was possible that it was waiting somewhere else or looking for the herd of geniuses. Then they started discussing who should sit in my car. Three girls entered but then they had a dilemma: which guy should get to ride with them. They started talking me into taking an extra passenger. I told them I wouldn't. It was very slippery and the drive was long, so I wouldn't take the risk. "Come on, please. You can put him in the trunk," the girls kept whining. Yes, of course, I will put him in the boot of the Hyundai like a dead hog. What the hell are you thinking with, I cursed to myself.

Finally I told them: "Okay, I'll take an extra passenger if you pay me 600 euros, because that's the fine for carrying too many people." That argument shut them up for good.

I let the meter tick until they argued for about 5-6 minutes. Finally they decided who got to ride with me and who went to the other taxi.

We finally got moving and drove east to **Espoo center** (about 9km) to a hot pub. Arriving there, one chick asked for my number so that I could pick them up and drive them back to their house. I told her I'd come if I was nearby. Actually I had no intention of carrying them anymore.

### The intensive "interrogation"

**December**. An evening on a regular weekday. **Matinkylä, southern Espoo**. A drunk woman with short hair, about 50-55 years old, got into my car behind the corner of a bar. She seemed Slavic by her looks and her accent. She had a guy with her, about 35 years old.

The couple got in and we drove to a neighboring district a few kilometers away.

The woman started to ask me questions from the back seat: "Are you from **Estonia**?" "Yes I am," I answered calmly and politely. She kept asking: "Do you know a taxi driver named Aivo?" "No, I don't," I again answered politely. She wasn't happy with my answers: "Do you wish to not speak to me?" I again told her calmly: "I can talk to you." I asked: "What do you want to talk about?" She kept on: "No-no-no, you don't want to talk to me."

I wasn't in the mood to argue with a drunk bonehead and kept it short: "Well, if you say so." She got heated: "Whoa-whoa-whoa!"

Then the guy tried to calm her: "Hey, stop babbling, what's your problem?" But she didn't listen to him. I laughed to that and told him: "Let it be, I see this ever night." He told me: "Yeah, Finns are like that, they like to tease but don't mean any harm by it."

I told the woman: "Sorry, forgive me, but we have nothing to talk about." She calmed down and explained: "I'm a bit drunk, I'm just teasing you." I told her: "I realized that. I see this every day." "Did you get it," she asked. "I got it," I answered. Then she started to apologize: "I'm sorry, I apologize for my actions and my words. I take them back." And then asked: "Wait, are you Aivo ("brain" in Finnish)?" I smirked and answered: "No, I'm not Aivo. Aivo was some acquaintance of yours." She kept at it: "Who are you then?" I told her: "That's not important." "Oh, that's not important," she agreed and added: "What's important is that you'd take me to **Kalastajanmäki**[48]." "Yes, exactly, that's important. Of course I will take you," I answered. She thanked me.

Why the hell are you annoying me then, if you don't mean any harm? Why do you want to pick a fight me and ruin my mood, if you don't mean any harm? Some kind of stressed and annoyed shitheads come to taxis to live out their disappointments and anger. If you're stressed, go train, go run, go have sex, drink wine, go take the edge off and do something pleasant, I was cursing to myself.

## "Turn the meter on if you want to fuck with us..."

**December**. The weekend. At about 7am I got a fare in **Leppävaara** district, on the border of **Helsinki** and **Espoo**, to an apartment building about a kilometer from the taxi stand.

The potential clients were a guy, about 25-30 years old, and a chick, about the same age. Dressed

---

[48]*Kalastajanmäki – a district in southern Espoo, next to the Matinkylä.*

simple, cheap, you could even say their clothes were "tired." They seemed pretty old and worn-out.

The couple came out of the doorway. They waved to signal me, that they are the ones who ordered the taxi. I waited for them to take a seat in the car. But they had other plans. They lit their cigarettes… What the fuck? I rolled down the passenger side window and asked: "What, are you going to smoke?" "Yes," the dude answered. What the fuck, I thought again. I told the guy: "While you're sucking on your cigarette, I'm going to start the meter." "Do it, if you want to fuck with us," the important gentleman told me. Exactly that. "Well, I don't know about fucking with you but if you've ordered a taxi, you have to pay for the waiting too," I said regarding the well-known rules. "Well you can always fuck with us if you want to," he repeated his view. The chick started laughing.

I told them what I thought about it: "Listen, I don't have the time to deal with you two." I rolled up the window and drove away. The two idiots kept staring, trying to figure out where I was going. To make it clear, I rolled down the window again and yelled: "You can order another taxi if you want to keep smoking your cigarettes!"

### The most important guys are the ones with the shortest stints

**October**. I couldn't get a break from the morons even on a Sunday evening. I picked up an oldman, about 55-60 years old, completely drunk, surprise-surprise. He came from a dive bar in **Matinkylä, southern Espoo**.

To reach the street from the bar, you have to go through a parking lot of an apartment building. They had even regulated which lane you can take depending on which way you were headed.

Because it was a Sunday evening and nobody was on the move anyway, I took the shortest route through the parking lot. That irritated my "important" client. He started to complain in a dry voice: "You're driving wrong." I asked "How am I driving wrong?" He repeated the same sentence: "You're driving wrong!" and added: "You can't drive like that." I asked again: "Where should I drive to get to the street?" The same story: "Well, you can't drive like that." I smirked and told him: "Well, this is the shortest route to your house right now." He could stop irritating me: "Still, you're driving wrong!" I got a bit angry with the complaining schoolgirl and answered: "Don't start any problems. It's a short drive (there was about 600-700m to go). I am taking you home on the shortest route and you're still bitching." He just smirked arrogantly sitting next to me. It was clear he enjoyed fucking with me.

*6. A street in Matinkylä. I took the "very important client" close by.*

We arrived in his yard. It was surrounded by three apartment buildings, in front of which was a U-shaped sidewalk. I asked him: "Which is your doorway?" There was a whole alphabet of them because the houses were all with the same number. The moron told me: "F." I asked: "Oh, F?" "F yeah, like a pharaoh," the moron emphasized. I asked: "Where is the F doorway exactly," so I would know where to go. He wasn't letting up: "I am the client, you should know, where I live!" I asked "Oh, now you're the important client, huh?" "Yes, I'm an important client, I'm very important," he kept bullshitting.

We were in front of the wrong door of the wrong house. I backed up 10 meters to his doorway and asked ironically: "Is it better now?" "Yes, now it's good, now it's very good," the idiot answered importantly. I asked: "Do you want the receipt?" "Yes, I do want the receipt." Yes, yes, for fuck's sake, here's your check. The bill was exactly 10 euros. 9 euros of it was the payment to start the drive so he drove for exactly 1 euro!

I was thinking to myself, what a douchebag, he gets home for 10 euros in rainy weather and you have to fuck with me.

### If you aren't using your turn signals, you need to signal with your finger

**October**. Afternoon. I was sitting at the taxi stand in **Tapiola, southeast Espoo**. I pushed the seat down to rest and watch some TV before another fare showed up.

I suddenly noticed from the side mirror that someone had walked to the back of the car. I didn't sit up right away and thought that someone had just passed the car. Suddenly a big round face like a full moon appeared behind the rear passenger window. He opened the door and asked if I was free. "Yes, I am," I told him. He told me: "I came to the car and thought there was no driver inside so I looked closer, that's why I was looking in the car, nose against the window."

The gentleman, about 30 years old, got in and I asked: "Where to?" He gave me the address. We had to go the border of **Helsinki-Vantaa**, about 17km away.

After a 15 minute drive we were almost there. We had about 1.5-2km to go.

We reached a spot where about 50 meters ahead of me there was a bus stopped in a bus stop, to let people on and off. I was doing 60-70km/h in a 70km/h zone. I looked and saw that the bus hadn't turned its left turning signal on so I decided to pass the bus. When I got to its rear end, it suddenly turned to the left, in front of me. I got past it, as I went to the oncoming lane. The bus driver sounded his horn from the back and flashed with his lights. I spoke out loudly, so the gentleman next to me heard me: "Why the fuck are you sounding the horn? You cut *me* off! Use your mirrors and turn signals, before you start making maneuvers!"

At the same time I lowered the side window and signaled to the bus driver using a sign that is known across the world to express what I thought about him and his maneuvers. The client agreed and seconded my signal.

# SHIT-FACED CLOWNS

## A crazed man in the middle of the road in a red jacket

I have collected stories about clients who weren't in an adequate condition when using my taxi. Some adventures are funny and pleasant. Some are unpleasant but unforgettable. Drunken people can get up to unbelievable things…

**December**. I was returning from **Haaga**[49] district in **West Helsinki**, where I had just dropped off a client. I was driving towards the city center of Helsinki, on **Mannerheimintie**[50], when suddenly a madman in a red jacket and some jeans jumped in front of me.

He ran into the middle of the street, stopped, stood with his feet apart and waved his arms crazily. He was trying to get me to stop my car. At first I thought it was a crazy drunk guy.

---

[49] *Haaga* – a district of Helsinki. It has 4 parts: South-Haaga, North-Haaga, Kivihaka and Lassila. It is located about 8km north of the city center.
[50] *Mannerheimintie* – the main street in Helsinki, about 5.5km long. It starts in the city center in Erottaja and ends where Vihdintie and Hakanmäentie streets cross, and where its name changes to Hämeenlinnänväylä.

I stopped the car at the side of the street and he wavered to the rear door. He rattled with it for a few moments, opened it and landed on the back seat. I realized that it was actually a very loud drunken woman.

After a few moments, when she had got her breathing and heart rate in order, she thanked me for stopping and picking her up. Like I had another choice. She then told me, still breathing heavily, that she wanted to go to the center of Helsinki, behind **Kamppi** center (about 3km). I asked her that does she want to get killed, running onto the street like that. To that the less-heavily breathing woman told me: "None of the taxis are stopping. Everybody is just passing by." I was thinking to myself, no wonder everybody's passing her if she's jumping into the street like a crazy person.

One thing was clear, there was nothing sensible going on in her head – she was under the influence of some heavy shit. She was yelling and screaming on the back seat the whole way. Then she explained to me and the whole world how tough she is, how much money she has and how she's going to a club to party.

About half a kilometer before arriving at the destination, she started asking me if I would go and have a coffee with her. And afterwards go out somewhere. I apologized politely that unfortunately I couldn't go because I was working, but maybe some other time. That answer didn't satisfy her so I added that I don't go out with clients. She asked again as we arrived. My continuous negative answer made her sad. She kept turning her dull eyes on me, in the rear view mirror, and then the street.

After floating in a mental space for a minute, I brought her back to reality and said: "Please pay the bill now. I have another client waiting, I have to go." I was actually lying about the client, I just wanted her out of the car. Also, I wanted to "free up" the register, because it was nighttime on a weekend and another fare could pop up any moment. Furthermore, I was hoping for a more pleasant client.

### Like an old soviet collective farmer

On one of the first nights when I was at the taxi stand in **Olari, southern Espoo**, I got a fare to a nearby pub. There are about 5 pubs in a 100 m radius of the taxi stand.

I drove in front of the pub shown in the order to wait for the client. In about 3 minutes two guys exited – a younger and an older guy. The last one reminded me of a real soviet collective farmer from the 1940s. He had a thick winter coat on and a furry hat, tilted to the side. Drunk of course, to make the "set" perfect.

They went their separate ways in front of the pub. The old man wiggled towards my car and asked through the window, stretching his words: "C-can I… Can I s-sit in the f-front?" I told him: "Sure you can, but you would have more room in the back." No, the old farmer still wanted to sit in the front. Well, if the client insists, what can you do?

I came out of the car, opened the passenger door for him, to get him in the car quicker and safer. I forgot to do one thing, though – to push the passenger seat back so that he would have more room. The front seat is usually pulled forward in Finnish taxis, because most of the clients wish to sit in the back. If it's pulled forward, you of course have more legroom in the back.

The farmer tried to get in the car, but the seat was so far forward and the backrest so up, that he couldn't fit at all. His head along with his furry hat had got stuck on the roof pillar. He squirmed how he could but he couldn't fit. I looked at the situation for a few moments and decided to lend a hand. I grabbed his head and pushed him in with brute force. He wasn't against it at all. He was satisfied to finally be resting on a soft seat. I closed the door after him and got in the car.

I asked him for the address of the destination. He wanted to go to his house, which was about 1.5km from the pub.

We were there in about three minutes. I stopped in a dark yard of an apartment building. The doorway was behind the corner, about 4-5 meters away, which I didn't see at first. So I told the old man: "Look out of the car, is it your place?" He only went: "Uhm, hum, doesn't seem like it." I told him: "Wait, I'll back up a bit so you could see it better." So I backed up about 10 meters and asked again: "Is it familiar?" "Oh yes, yes, this is my house. Thank you," he suddenly became happy. Then his vision became even clearer. He was able to guide me to his doorway, on the other side of the house.

I drove in front of his door and he paid the bill. I helped him out of the car to the door. I waited for a minute to see if he gets in the house and doesn't stay outside in the cold. In Finland, it's the duty of the taxi driver to make sure that the client gets to a warm room before leaving. The old man did good considering his condition. I left to transport more clowns.

## The "bomber" with the plastic bag

A few days later there was a similar situation. I was at the taxi stand in **Olari** again, when I got an order to the same address, but to the pub next door, in the end of the cross street. There are three pubs on the short street.

I was just backing up to the door of the pub so the client would easily get to the car. To make sure I didn't hit anyone, I was looking in the mirrors. In one of the mirrors I noticed how a very-very-very drunk male, carrying a plastic bag in both his hands, dashed out of the pub door. He would have made a decent mad bomber. I was so amazed by the scene that I stopped backing up and kept looking in the mirror to see, which side he was trying to enter the car from.

But the Bomber didn't reach the car at first. I saw in the mirror how his feet and plastic bags raised high up in the air and how he then smashed into the ground, headfirst.

I quickly exited the car to see if he was all right after such a hit. I asked if he could move and if anything was broken. To my concerns, he calmly answered: *"Ei oo mitään, kaikki on hyvin. Mennään nyt kotiin[51]."* "No selvä juttu[52]," I told him. I helped him up and picked up both of his bag from the very slippery yard and put them in the back seat.

The bomber got in the car, so I asked the logical question, where was he going.

Like the alcohol wasn't enough, I think the fall had damaged his ability to speak quite a bit. I didn't understand anything he was saying about the destination. His tongue was soft as hell. I heard something like Mittaarikatu. To be sure, I asked again in a loud voice: "Was it Mittarikatu?" "No-no," the bomber stretched out and tried to repeat the address again. I still didn't get what he was saying. This time I thought I had heard something like Meettorikatu. I asked for a third time: "Was it Meettorikatu or something like that?" After the third time he got angry. He collected himself and tried hard and loud: "Mmmmeeedddeeeooriigadduuu." "Oh, **Meteoorikatu**[53]. Got it! Thank you," I told the just-shot-down bomber. "Now I understand where you want to go," I calmed him down, telling him the situation was under control and I knew where to take him. I was

---

[51] *"Oh it's nothing, everything is well. Let's go home now!"*
[52] *"Understood!"*
[53] *"Meteor street."*

thinking to myself, that he was a meteor himself as he was flying down the street. You need a good frame to be able to take these kinds of hits. The dents will show the next morning.

### The "submarine" that was hit by a torpedo

**November**. An evening on a workday. I got a fare from a bar in **Kivenlahti, southwest Espoo**. Because the evening had been quiet, of course I headed to pick up the client to get some money in the register, not knowing what I had coming.

The order was about 100 meters from a bar. Next to that bar, there are actually two other bars. If I had analyzed the information in my head, I would have known that the client must have a problem walking.

I arrived at the bars and waited for the next "airplane" to exit the bars. "Airplanes" are drunk people who need to walk with their hands up to maintain balance.

You wouldn't believe how drunk this guy was! He couldn't stand up by himself. The barman sat him on the back seat of the car. I asked the barman where the airplane was headed. He didn't know. I asked the drunkard for his address. He told me a word like a stretched out tape. It sounded like **Allveelaevakatu**[54] street. It sounded logical, considering that I was in Kivenlahti on a street whose name was sea themed. He looked like a submarine that had been hit by a torpedo, not an airplane. He added that he would guide me to the right place.

Okay. Deal. I got in the car and we started driving to the destination with the "damaged vessel."

Basically we drove out of the yard across the street. We went to a yard that was between some apartment buildings. The road was twisted like a snake. And it was very narrow. It was a sidewalk, which had snow walls on the side of it, about a meter tall. He told me the number of the house but I didn't see it. Like always, there were no numbers, not on the doorways, not on the houses.

Because it was slippery and narrow, I slowly drove up a hill between the houses, looking for the right one. I asked multiple times where his house was. Was this familiar? Should I stop there or there? He didn't react. I thought his house would come later.

---

[54] *"Submarine street."*

After cruising up the hill for a few minutes, the drunkard suddenly realized that we had driven past his house.

Of course I got annoyed. I had to reverse for about 10 meters on this very slippery, very narrow road. When backing up, I saw some residents of the houses walking their dog. I stopped the car and asked them: "Where is house number ... ?" It turned out to be back down the hill.

In the meantime, the drunkard had opened the car door and started to leave the car. He probably thought he had magically regained his ability to walk. I told him to close the door before it got stuck in the snow wall. I asked him to wait before exiting and told him: "Wait for a minute, I'll back up a little closer, or you won't reach the house." I backed up for about a meter and he insisted: "That's enough! I want to go out now!" I stopped the car and told him: "Okay, pay the bill. After you do that, I'll help you get inside."

Because I had driven with him for a long time, reversing and looking for the house, the meter had ticked to 14 euros. The starting fee was 9 euros, because it was after 8pm. I told him the amount, to which he started to bitch: "Why so much? Damn, you're greedy!"

After about a minute of slow-motion searching, he found 12 euros in his pockets. I told him that he needs 2 euros more, to which he started protesting that he doesn't have any and he wouldn't give any more. I thought, fuck it, I have wasted so much time – I'll throw him out of the car, help him to the house so that he wouldn't get stuck in the cold and drive away.

There was about 10 meters to the house from the car. I carried the soft "submarine" to the doorway. He held on to me so tightly that the seams on my jacket were breaking.

When we got to the house, I asked him for his keys. I looked for them in all of his pockets but didn't find them. I searched through his pockets as well, but I couldn't find them either. Only a crumbled 20-euro bill came out of one of the pockets. I told him: "See, you have money pay the bill!" "No I won't," he said, at the same time taking the bill back. I thought, fuck him, just open the door so I could get out of here. How much time could I waste?

We searched through his pockets once more but still didn't find any keys. Then I saw someone moving in the hallway and asked him to open the door.

The young man opened the door from the inside and I could enter the building with the drunkard. We went a floor higher to an apartment door. Then it turned out that it wasn't his apartment, they only kept his keys there. He lived 1.5 floors down from that apartment, so basically in the basement.

I took the guy, unable to walk by himself, down the stairs to his door. I opened the door for him, threw his bag in and told him good-bye.

Out of the house, I started swearing loudly over a fare like this. There was one more surprise though. When I checked the back seat to see if the drunkard had left something behind, I discovered that the seat was wet. The fucking moron had pissed himself and ruined the seat.

Fuck, that killed my mood completely. First you search for a completely fucked up client's house for 6-7 minutes, then you have to get the money owing douchebag to his house, which takes another 10 minutes, so that he wouldn't freeze and then you discover that the fucker has pissed in your car...

I decided to never take a client from that address. I drove there back once more, right then. I told the barman: "This is the last fucking time you call a taxi for one of these imbeciles! Just call the police next time!" To explain my aggressiveness, I explained that the idiot had ruined my back seat and pissed in my car. He looked confused. "Yeah, this is the first time that your clients have left in this condition," I commented on his expression and left the bar.

## The old folks who had gotten drunk in the early evening

**April**. It was about 6pm. I was cruising in **Espoo center** district, in **Mid-Espoo**. Well if you want adventures, then this is the pace.

I got a fare to a "fun" pub named M… & Hanna. I took an old woman who was completely drunk to a nearby apartment building. Again, it was just 6pm.

I drove to her doorway where she paid the bill. I opened the car door to get her out quicker and that she would leave. Of course she thought that I was extremely polite and giving her royal service. She almost fainted thanking me multiple times for the great service. I finally got rid of her and turned back towards Espoo center.

The circus continued. Right away, I got a fare to the same bar.

I drove there and saw the security guard outside with an old man. The man was completely plastered. He was leaning on the security guard. What the hell started happening then – first he didn't realize that the taxi had arrived. I told the guard: "Next time don't order a taxi, call the police. They need to get sober, don't put them on a taxi. We aren't a sobering house. But okay, I'll take the drunkard this time."

I asked the old man: "What's your address?" "Blablabla," was all that sounded from the back seat. I couldn't understand shit. Fuck! I was slowly going, he suddenly babbled: "Turn right here!" I asked, a bit startled: "From here? Already?" We had driven for about 200 meters. "Yeah yeah," he babbled: "Here, yes. "For fuck's sake.

I drove to his door and stopped so he could pay his bill. I don't remember the exact number but it was probably about 6 euros, because the starting tax was 5.70 euros and drive was only about 200 meters long.

I was waiting for him to give me a card or cash to pay the bill. He was looking for a card. First he offered me a fucking library card. I told him: "That isn't it." Then he offered me a work ID. I told him: "This isn't it either." Then I saw his card in his wallet. I told him: "See, THIS is the right one," pointing to a specific card. The drunkard tried to get it from his wallet with his fat fingers but he couldn't.

We had been sitting for 4-5 minutes. I was tired of waiting, I had had enough. I offered to help him and to take the card out myself. He agreed. I got the card, put it in the card reader and gave it to the drunkard to enter his PIN.

The moron was able to enter the wrong code twice. I told him: "Tell me the code, I'll enter it myself." "No, I won't!" he got irritated. Finally I had had enough and told him: "Get out of the car!" I've wasted 10 minutes waiting with this moron in front of his house, the bill is 6 euros and that fucking asshole couldn't even pay that. How long can you suffer?

He didn't understand why I was so angry. I came out of the car, opened his door and ordered him to exit. "QUICKLY!" I yelled. He still wished to pay. I told him in three languages: "*Poshjol nahhui*[55] from this car! *Nopeasti!*[56]"

He finally wiggled out of the car. I slammed the door close and started to get in the car when he was still babbling something. I asked him: "What problem do you have?" He still didn't have any problems. Well I had one, because I just wasted useless time on a drunkard who wasn't able to pay the bill.

---

[55] *"Get lost!" in Russian.*
[56] *"Quickly!"*

I cancelled the fare and drove away from Espoo center to avoid other clowns and the freeloaders that were eating my nerves.

### Which body is stronger – a Hyundai's or a Finn's?

Late **May**. A bit after midnight, I came to work from watching football at "home". I got a fare from **Saunalahti** district, in **southwest Espoo**, next to **Kivenlahti**. I picked up an old couple, about 60 years old, who wanted to go to just a few kilometers west, to **Kauklahti** (about 5km).

The old man was hammered as hell. After they paid their bill in front of their house, when he was climbing out of the car, he lost his balance and slammed into the side of the car and disappeared onto the tarmac. Fortunately it seemed like the woman had had practice lifting him. She helped him up and helped him to the door. There wasn't a dent on the car, though. This time the Hyundai's body had been stronger than the Finnish man's.

### The female tornado

On a Friday evening in **May** at about 10pm, I got a good fare and a client from a neighborhood of private houses in **southwest Espoo**.

I drove to a private house. I stopped on the street and waited for the client. In about a minute I saw a "tornado" getting closer to the car from the right side. It turned out to be a drunk woman in about her thirties. I decided to open the rear door from the inside for her, just in case, so that she wouldn't run into the car.

First she landed in the back seat on her side. When she finally sat up in the middle of the seat, she told me, searching for eye contact in the mirror: "I would l-like to go to Ooolarrriii." "Where to in **Olari**?" I asked right away. Then I specified: "Do you want to go to the center?" "Y-y-yesss, riiight to the cennnteerr," the lady answered. She then asked: "H-howwmuchhh to Olarrrii?" "Well it's about 6km so it's about 18 euros," I speculated. She then took her wallet and investigated its contents, then showed them to me. It only had a few coins in it. She asked me if I could count the money. I told her: "No, I am not looking in your wallet. See for yourself how much you got in there." I think that sobered her up for a moment. He searched through her wallet once more and admitted: "H-heyy, I h-have to g-get more." She exited the car and hobbled back to the house, which was about 30-35 meters away.

She was absent for about 3 minutes and then I saw her staggering back to the car. Near the finish line she jumped on the back seat, head first, hitting her head on the other door. She sat up, again, looking at me in the rear view mirror and told me: "N-noww w-we can g-go. I n-now h-have enoughhh money." I then told her: "Maybe you should close the door before we go. I think it's safer that way." To my request, she closed the door like she was trying to pull it through the car. I commented: "Hey, this isn't a tractor where you have to close the doors with force." "Oh-h, I, I'm s-sorry," was the stuttering answer from the calmed down Tornado.

We started driving to Olari and she started worrying again: "Hey, h-how much will the b-bill be? D-do I h-have enough money?" I was trying to calm her down: "Don't worry, it's only about 18 euros." Then she changed the subject completely and started asking me if I was religious and where I was from. I answered her politely, to which she completely shut down and was quiet for a minute. Then she started again: "A-actually I don't r-really k-know m-myself what I'm t-thinking, or what t-to say o-or to a-ask." She seemed pretty confused.

Going forward she had a new interesting topic. She asked me: "Hheyy, what kind of ccaaar is thiiis?" I told her: "Guess." "Ooooh, whennn I lookkkatt the signnn in the front, IlikkeaaMerc?" the woman guessed. "Good job, that's right!" I praised the lady. She was still going on: "Inntteressting, it doesn't jumpp on thheroooad at all." To that, I commented: "Of course it doesn't. It's a Merc, not a bicycle." The topic had ended and we were quiet for a few minutes.

When we had about 5 minutes to go to Olari, Ms. Tornado started talking again: "Yyouknooww, **Rami**[57] is sinnnging there tonnighhhtt." "Got it," was the only thing I answered and to specify, I asked: "Where is he singing exactly?" She didn't know. "Let's go to thh-hecenntteerr and thhennwe'lllllfinddd out, whhher-reexactllyyy," the Tornado came up with a plan.

So we got to Olari center. I asked her again, where she wants to go, which bar Rami was performing at. The bars were on either side of the street. She

---

[57]***Rami*** – *a Finnish singer*

still didn't have an answer and suggested going left. So I turned left to the taxi stop and stopped between to pubs. She then asked me: "Hhhey, whichhh pub is Rami singinggg in tonigghttt, do you knnnoww?" I told her again: "I really don't know. Go outside and yell RAMI-RAMI, WHERE ARE YOU?"

She paid the bill, left the car and right away started waving her arms in the middle of the sidewalk and yelling: "Rammmiiii, whheeereeeaaaaareeyouuuu???"

## "Usually the taxi driver drives a part of the trip for free"

**September**. A late evening on a Saturday. I took 2 older guys, in their 50s, and a younger guy, about 20-22 years old, from a "hot" bar in **Kivenlahti, southwest Espoo** to **Helsinki**. The younger dude started bullshitting right away, and asked me: "Don't you speak Finnish?" I answered him, astonished: "I do, don't you understand my Finnish?" "Oh, you do, yes," he apologized. He started asking about my car: "Is the Merc a good car?" I answered him: "You're not in a Merc, you're in a Hyundai." "Is that right?" he was wondering. "Yes it is," I told him. He made me laugh.

About 10 kilometers before Helsinki, he started talking: "Up in **Tornio**[58], the taxi drivers stop the meter when the taxi is near to the destination." I think he thought it would be a good time to stop it 10 kilometers before arriving to Helsinki. I told him: "Maybe in Tornio, but here in Helsinki or Espoo we don't do that," and asked: "how would we get paid then?" "What pay," he asked. I told him again: "How would we get paid if we let the client go for free for half the way. We get paid a per cent of the money clients pay us." To that he thought that taxi drivers get enough money to sometimes drive for free. I asked him: "Do you work for free?" He didn't know what to say and was quiet.

At the meantime, the older generation in the back decided to let everybody know that they're there. They started arguing loudly if they would stay in the center of Helsinki or if they would go further, to North-Helsinki. I interfered right away: "I'm taking you to the city center and you can take another taxi there, if you want to move on." I had had enough of the drunk, unreal party after 10 minutes.

---

[58]***Tornio*** - *a town located 375 kilometers north of Helsinki.*

*7. Helsinki's Central Railway Station. Around it there are several popular bars, pubs and nightclubs.*

Then the younger guy started questioning me again: "Where would you recommend us to go party?" I told him: "All the bars are open, you can go to all of them." "No-no, we want a place where there would be young people," he didn't give up. I suggested "Mallones," to which he came up with the "Milli Club." I agreed and told him: "Yeah, that's a great place! You should go there for sure. You can even get in at 7am!" "Do 19 year-olds get in," he kept asking. To get rid of them quickly, I told him: "They will, for sure."

We arrived at the club. They exited and I drove off. At the next light I looked at the back seat to see if maybe something was left behind. They did leave something – a big, worn Samsung, which would have been good for cracking nuts and a lighter. I thought to myself after seeing the "merchandise": "There's nothing to do with the phone, but at least I won't have to buy matches for some time."

### A very tired gentleman from the forest of Siuntio

**June**. Weekend. It was 6am. I was sitting at the taxi stand in **Kivenlahti, southwest Espoo** and waiting for the morning ETL[59], to get to the airport and then end my round. Because there was another hour until the ETL, I wanted to get a quick fare. I decided to go on a little adventure to fight my boredom and sleepiness.

I saw multiple times that there was an unfilled order in **Kirkkonummi**, about 11 kilometers west of Kivenlahti. The client would have gone back to **Helsinki** to the train station. It would have been a trip worth 55 euros. A bit less than the airport but I could rest sooner. And the trip from the train station to Kivenlahti was shorter too.

---

[59]*ETL – in Finnish: "ennakkotilaus," pre-order*

First I thought I shouldn't go because it was too far. But when it had been up there for over 20 minutes, I took the risk and headed towards Kirkkonummi.

On the way, another order appeared on the list. But when I got to Kirkkonummi, both of them were gone – someone had taken them. I thought – well that's great, I drove 11 kilometers and lost both orders. So I went to the taxi stand in the Kirkkonummi train station. I analyzed my actions and thought what to do next.

After having a calming cigarette, I sat back in the car and looked what was happening on Data. I noticed there was another fare "close" to me – about 15 minutes away. It showed the destination and that trip would have been worth it. At the same time, the client was far enough that the calling center would have cursed at me – because another taxi might have been closer and could have got it faster. It was 14 kilometers away. I didn't dare to take the order myself.

I drove off the taxi stand and decided that if I'm at the bridge and the order is still there, I would take it and get them. On the bridge I had two choices – if the fare wouldn't be there, I would turn east, towards Kivenlahti. And if it was there, I would turn west.

I reached the bridge. Turning left, to the highway, I would have gotten back to Kivenlahti and turning right, I would get the order – which was in **Siuntio** county woods, even more to the west.

Unexpectedly an order did pop up – it was the same one, still untaken somewhere in a forest in Siuntio. I had never been to that area.

The order had the client's phone number but I thought I would use it when I got closer. Either way, I decided to get the order, to see what kind of a place it was. Even if I don't get the client this time, then the next time I'll know what place is it and how to get there. I had nothing better to do anyway.

I drove towards the given address. The highway turned to a smaller road and that turned into a forest road, which only had a single lane in the end. A wall of fog also greeted me, which got thicker every kilometer.

When there was about 5 minutes to go on the navigation, I took the order. I called the client to ask if the car is still needed. They did. Good news! At least it's sure that I get out of these unknown woods, better yet, I'm going to get paid for it.

*8. The vision of the gentleman picked up was probably as foggy. On the way from Siuntio to Helsinki.*

Finally I reached the end of the forest road. There was a villa on the rocky shores of the bay. There wasn't anyone waiting or moving near the house. I decided to leave the car and check the house, to see what was going on.

When I exited the car, I was greeted by thick foggy rain – like foam was raining on me. As I got closer to the house, I saw that it was on a high rock right on the edge of the sore. That's why there was thick fog and the foamy rain. All that humidity coming from the sea.

I found two gentlemen in the house, about 50 years old. They were drinking cognac and talking. I asked if they had ordered the taxi. It turned out that they had. One of them told me that the client would arrive right away.

The client was a gentleman who seemed very tired on this early hour. I could see that an adventurous night had been gone through. He reminded me of a 90s heavy metal band's singer.

After about 5 minutes he took a seat in the back. I asked him for the address and we got moving.

The GPS showed 40 minutes to the destination. The man "parked" himself between the seatbelt, what turned out to be a smart choice, considering the following drive.

We managed to drive a few kilometers when I heard a weird sound from the back. I glanced back and saw how the gentleman had rested his head on the side window and was snoring through his mouth.

After about 20 kilometers, when I had to turn on the **Kehä II**[60] circuit from the highway, I noticed how he plunged from right to left in the rear view mirror. He woke up for a moment, checked where he was from the window and fell back asleep. As I needed to board

---

[60]*Kehä II - In the region of Espoo is one of the major highways in Finland, . The road runs north-south, connecting Turuntie in the north, to Länsiväylä in the south.*

the ship from Helsinki to Tallinn the same morning, I was in a hurry. I had to "shorten" the 40-minute trip.

When I turned on the circuit, and again when I turned towards **Tapanila**[61] district, the same thing happened – the man woke up for a second and then fell asleep again. For the rest of the way, the man just snored and slept through the whole trip. When I turned towards Tapanila, I was greeted by three *jackasses* by the road. They were standing in their colorful underwear and having a cigarette. I guess they were enjoying the summer morning and the wet grass.

When I got to the client's house, about 50 meters to go, I woke him up. I asked him: "Is this the right place?" He looked around but didn't say anything. I asked again: "Well, is it familiar?" "Yes, yes-yes, now it is, yeah," was the sleepy answer.

He handed me his card after looking for it for a few minutes and paid the bill. I asked him: "Do you need the receipt and do you want me to write the start and the destination of the trip on it?" "Yes, give it, yeah," the man was still sleepy.

The old man looked at the receipt, looked at me and asked: "How much did the trip cost now?" I told

---

[61]*Tapanila* - *a district of private houses in Helsinki, about 17 kilometers northeast of the city center.*

him: "92.80 euros," and added, just in case: "The trip was 57 kilometers long." "Oh, okay," he said, looked at the check for a few moments, put it in his pocket and left the car, wishing me a good day.

### Well, of course – come and puke in the car!

**June**. Evening on a regular workday. I had just taken a cute lady to a nightclub in **Helsinki**. I picked up another client right in front of the club. It was a pretty drunk but decent gentleman. He wanted to go to **Kirkkonummi**, about 30km west of Helsinki. I was fine with that, because I got nearer to **Espoo** and got paid for it.

He got in the car and when we got out of the city, on the highway, he got tired and fell asleep, his head against the rear window.

On the **Kehä III**[62] circuit, when the navigation showed about 5 minutes to go, the gentleman for some reason suddenly woke up. At the same moment he threw up. Most of the "soup" went on the floor and

---

[62]*Kehä III – a 46km long circuit in southern Finland crossing Kirkkonummi, Espoo, Helsinki and Vantaa areas, connecting Länsiväylä, Turunväylä, Hämenlinnanväylä, Tuusulanväyä and Porvoonväylä motorways.*

into his own lap, but some was on the seat, the door and in the door pocket.

I stopped the car on the side of the road and told him to get out of the car in case more of the barf needed to be discharged. He got out of the car and seemed startled by the situation. I asked him to clean his clothes, as well as the door and the seat. I gave some paper towels and cleanser from the boot.

Then I started asking him to pay for the damages, because I couldn't pick up any more clients with a car like that.

First I had to clean the car from the puke as well as the smell. I demanded 200 euros from him, which he didn't accept. I thought, okay, let's do 150, I could get it cleaned pretty quickly.

After arguing for some time, when I had threatened him with the police, we agreed to a hundred, which he had to pay extra to the 50-euro bill. I offered to take him home but he wished to walk the last kilometer in fresh air. So we went our separate ways on the circuit. He marched right over the ditch and through the bushes towards his house. I drove back to **Kivenlahti** (about 10km) to clean the car in the car wash.

### Mister Piss-stream

**July**. Monday night. There were many people on the loose, some wasted on alcohol, others on antidepressants. I picked up a bewildered guy in the **Tapiola** post in **southeast Espoo**. Before sitting in the taxi, he went and took a high-arced piss on an illuminated commercial banner in front of me. After the golden shower, he sat in the car and told me he wanted to go to **Viikkari**. I asked: "What the hell is a Viikkari?" "Oh, you don't know??" Mister Piss-stream wondered. "Don't you know Viking Arms?" It turned out to be a pub in **Laajahti** district, near Tapiola (about 3km). Fuck, they have a slang word for everything. Viikkari, Mäkkäri[63], täppäri[64], läppäri[65]...

He clearly wasn't right in his head because the whole way to Viikkari he was acting like he would hit me. I looked to see what the hell was he wrestling back there. He explained: "Don't be afraid, I'm not going to really hit you, I'm just joking..." Well, great: Finnish "jokers" moving around on a Monday night.

---

[63]*Mäkkäri* – *McDonald's in Finnish slang*
[64]*Täppäri* – *tablet in Finnish slang*
[65]*Läppäri* – *laptop in Finnish slang*

## A collision with tarmac does not ruin a man

**July**. Midnight on a regular workday. I was sitting in **southwest Espoo**, at the taxi rank in **Soukka**, waiting for an order. Right across the street there was a pub. I have not seen anyone coming out of there just lightly drunk, always heavily intoxicated.

This time I saw a gentleman, in his 40s or 50s wearing a light jacket and jeans. He flew out of the bar door like a rocket and made contact with a birch tree in front of the stairs. He wasn't just drunk, I think he was testing the limits of how drunk one can be. All the objects one could lean on for support and move on, he used a hundred and one percent to stay up.

After getting his strength together leaning on the tree, he had a plan where to go next. He grabbed a handrail next to him. Then he smoothly moved on to a house wall, leaning on it with two hands, face towards the wall. Then he turned his face to the street to cross it. The rocket pushed himself off of the wall and grabbed an electrical post right next to him. Then, after a time of summoning his strength again, he stumbled across the street, finding a traffic sign for support. He then proceeded to move in a way which can't be considered walking, to the next electrical post and to the glass wall of a bus stop.

I observed this and wondered if he would really try to enter my car and go somewhere with his remaining wisdom? Considering the experience I had with the kind of customers who don't know who they are, where they are and where they want to go, added to the fact that they usually can't find money or they don't have it at all, it seemed safer to leave the post. But before that I wanted to make sure if he REALLY wanted to get into my car. So I stayed on the post, watching what would happen next.

And the fellow came to my car and started to open the rear door but I had locked the doors. He tried to open the door. Failing to do so and not realizing why he couldn't succeed, I lowered the window and told him "You're not getting in my car, you're too drunk." I don't need a customer who has problems standing up or paying for the ride. Or worse, he could throw up in the car. Then my round would be ruined for a couple of hours along with my mood.

He didn't understand that he couldn't get in the car, and continued pulling on the door. So I slowly started driving, so that he would let go of the door. He did and looked for support on the trunk door with his left hand, which probably would leave a dent on the car because of his loose control of his body. So I accelerated a little more and he only slightly grazed the back end of my car. He then lost his balance and fell on the tarmac face down behind the car. I saw it in my rear view mirror and heard the thump. It must have been very painful.

I left the post, turned in front of the pub and stopped across the street. I stayed to see if he would move or if I needed to call the ambulance.

After recovering for about 30 seconds, he turned on his back. Then, after a minute he was sitting up, enjoying the dusky summer evening. He was feeling good enough to light a cigarette he found in his pocket.

The stuntman's face seemed OK, so I guess the hit wasn't that bad. But I think his body would remind him of the hit the next day. Seeing that he was OK, I left the post to the nearby **Espoonlahti** post.

## The annoying drunk old man and the guy running in circles

Early **July**. It was after 2am. I picked up an old woman and an old man, both drunk as hell, from a pub in **Haukilahti, southern Espoo**. The old girl wanted to go off earlier, in the same area. The man wanted to go to **Matinkylä** (about 2km).

I turned on the street from the yard of the old lady and started to drive towards Matinkylä. Suddenly the old man started yelling: "Where the hell are you going now?" I calmly answered: "To **Nelikkotie**[66]." "No, Nelikkotie is the other way," the confused gray man kept moaning. There was only a forest the other way, because we were in the end of a street. I asked the fossil: "Do you even know where we are going or where your house is?" After thinking for a moment he agreed: "Oh, yeah, we can't go that way." Damn imbecile.

We arrived at his house. The bill was 18 euros. For some reason he wanted to leave a tip of 2 euros. He told me: "Let's make it 20 euros." I just wanted to get rid of him because there was a pop-up on Data that said that close by, at the taxi stand in **Olari** there's a client who needs a taxi. I wanted to get the new client, but no. He kept fiddling around, still wanting to leave me a tip. Finally when he started to look for his money, he couldn't find his wallet for the first few minutes. I was practically boiling inside, because I

---

[66]*A street in Matinkylä*

was thinking I need to drive him back to where I picked him up, if he doesn't have his wallet.

Finally he managed to find it and paid the bill. He still didn't want to leave the car. I had had enough. I exited and pulled him out of the rear door and escorted him to the house. I put him leaning on the wall so that he wouldn't fall in his condition. When I had put his hands against the wall like a fugitive I told him: "You should be safer here. The wall will keep you up now."

I left and flew back to Olari to get the client waiting at the taxi stand but I didn't get it. Another taxi turned there a moment before me and took the customer. I was cursing to myself – that's what you get when you deal with these drunkards. They waste your time and then you miss out on the next client.

I drove back to Matinkylä and went back at the taxi stand. There was some "life" in a bus stop in front of me. A madman, clearly not sober, ran circles in the bus stop. He ran diagonally for about 10 meters to one direction, then turned round and ran the other way for the same distance. He did this non-stop. His trajectory got so wide at one point that he almost ran into a shop of eyeglasses, head first. Maybe that would have helped him – fixed his vision or something. Fortunately he just grazed the window of the shop. I looked at the crazed man and thought that some people have interesting hobbies to practice on summer mornings.

After a few moments I got a fare and had to leave the circus. I didn't see the ending of the play that time…


## "I'll "park" my bike and then we'll be right there"

**July**. Early morning on a workday. It was about 5am. I was a part of a tragic comedy once again.

A fare appeared on Data. It was in **Olari** district in **southern Espoo**. When I got there, I tried to get as close as I could to the doorway, so that the client could easily get in and wouldn't have to walk. I had to drive up a steep hump. The rear-wheel driven Merc didn't want to go up the rubbly hump, though, and I got stuck on it.

After wiggling for a bit, I got unstuck and up the hill after wasting some nerves. I stopped next to the doorway, where it was very narrow. There was a metal handrail to the left of me, behind it a drop of about 3 meters. To the right of me, there was the house.

I wanted to reverse in front of the doorway so that when the client comes, we could safely drive down the hill. I wiggled again with my luxury car and finally I managed to park like I had planned. As it turned out, all that fucking around was useless.

The car parked, I called the client to say I had arrived. I was hoping for a stint to the airport with a decent gentleman and I could end my round with a well-paying fare. Usually taxis are ordered for these kinds of stints at those times.

I called three times, but every time it went into voicemail. I left a message that I was there and waiting in front of the doorway. A minute later a drunk bonehead called me back and asked me: "Where are you?" I told him: "I'm in front of the doorway, behind the house." "Where?" he couldn't understand. I explained again: "I'm in front of the E doorway." "No-no-no, come to the Olarius bar!" he ordered me on the other side of the line. I asked: "What do you mean Olarius? The car was ordered here!" "Well yeah, but we already walked to the bar," the drunk imbecile explained.

I circled through the narrow sidewalks between the apartment buildings for a few hundred meters until I got to the bar. A couple of drunk guys, both about

40-45 years old, met me there. They were completely wasted. One of them had an old bicycle with him. After seeing my face, he tried to calm me down: "No, I'm not taking the bike. I'll park it here somewhere." Hearing the info, his friend took the poor bike and threw it over a 1.5-meter-high fence to some bushes.

I looked at what had happened and the only thing I could think was: "Oh, that's how you park. Got it. Next time I'll know."

With the bike "safely parked," the men entered the car. The man I spoke on the phone with sat next to me, and the cyclist got in the back. Again, both were completely wasted, almost in a coma.

They started to talk about what had happened in the bar. It turned out that their friend had gotten in a fight and had apparently lost it. Halfway to **Helsinki**, where they still wanted to go to a bar, they had a fight. The man on the phone was angry at the cyclist because he didn't try to break up the fight. The cyclist hadn't realized that there had been a fight going on at all. They kept yelling at each other over the same topic for half the drive.

We finally arrived in Helsinki. The guys wanted to go to an entertainment building across the street from the train station. They really seemed like they needed more entertainment and action. There was a problem when it was time to pay the bill, though. They started arguing again about who should pay the bill. The man on the phone thought that the cyclist would pay and vice versa. The cyclist had an argument – he said he had already paid for the drinks and smokes in the last bar. They kept bouncing the payment from one to the other. Finally I had had enough and shouted: "Just decide, who'll pay! I don't have all day to listen to your arguing." The guy on the phone looked for his wallet, took out his card and paid the bill.

The clowns went to the bar and I headed back to Espoo. What a morning, I thought. All kinds of weird people moving around. Another 13-hour chapter of the theatre of life had ended and I could rest again.


### "I don't know who I am, where I'm going and what my PIN is."
**July**. A weeknight. I picked up an old drunk, about 55-60 years old, from the taxi stand in **Espoo center, Mid-Espoo**. I took him to a small neighborhood called **Rihvelmäki**, which was nearby (about 2.5 km). When arriving, it turned out that he doesn't have any money on him. He promised to get some from inside.

He exited the car and went straight to the doorway next to the car. He tried to get in but didn't succeed. He didn't have the key or the code. After trying, he came back to the car and said he would pay by card. Of course he didn't remember the PIN. We still managed to pay the bill because the card reader recommended using the magnetic stripe on the back of the car. During the payment, the guy kept worrying how he could get in his house. He explained, that he actually lived in the next row house, about 50 meters away, not in the one he just tried to get into. Anyway he wasn't really sure where he had to go.

He thought he should climb a window to get inside. He asked me if I would help him. I refused. I left him to deal with his problem and drove away.

After that fare I left Espoo center to avoid future "adventures." I went to the taxi stand in **Olari, southern Espoo**. Not that there would be less "adventurers" there. Moments before arriving at the taxi stand, another taxi took a spot in front of me to take a client, but he didn't take him.

There was a wasted old man sitting on a bench there. After seeing the first taxi, he hopped up, but lost his balance and fell straight back to the bench. He almost fell over the bench but managed to stop. When he saw me, he did the same but I drove past him too.

The taxi in front of me left and went to look for a treasure somewhere else. I went to the taxi stand again to investigate how drunk the old man was. Maybe I could pick him up and earn some money.

I stopped in front of him and he got up. This time he managed to hold his balance. He took two steps and stopped right next to the car. I opened the door from the inside. He just fell in the car, back first, his head landed almost in my lap.

After he straightened himself I asked where he was headed. He wanted to go to **Tapiola** (about 4km). As he wasn't in any kind of shape, I asked him just to be sure, if he had money to pay me. He told me he did. I asked him to show me, to which he just said: "I do, I do." I repeated: "Show me." He still went: "I have it, I have it." Again, I repeated myself: "Just show me the money, I'm not going anywhere until I'm sure you have money for the drive." He took his wallet from his inner pocket and showed me his debit card.

I agreed to get going. I asked him for the exact address. First I heard something like "Dakkulantie." I searched for it in the navigation but didn't find anything. I asked him to say the street name again. He answered with a soft, dry voice: "Dakkojantie." I searched for that, but still came up empty. I decided to enter the first three letters to see what the navigation would recommend. I entered "Tak," to which the navigation offered me "**Takojantie**[67]." I asked the old man if "Takojantie" was correct. "Yes, Takojantie, yes," he got ecstatic. We had finally found the right address.

I took him to a dark parking lot between some apartment buildings. He didn't want to stop in front of his doorway, he wished to stretch his legs and walk to the house from the parking lot. When I was stopping the car, he started to put his card, which he had held in his hand the whole way, back in his pocket. I told him: "Don't put the card away, we are going to need it in a bit."

I took the card and entered it to the terminal. I gave it to the old man to enter his PIN.

He entered the code. I pressed OK but the payment didn't go through. I told him: "You entered the wrong code, try again." He took the terminal. I saw how he pressed 3, 9, 5, at the same time pronouncing loudly – nine, nine, five. I told him that he didn't press

---

[67]*A street in Tapiola district*

nine, he pressed three and asked: "Don't you remember the code?" "I do, I do," he confidently answered. Again, he pressed three and said nine. I told the old man again: "The button you pressed isn't NINE, it's THREE," and added: "nine is in the low corner, three is in the upper corner."

I told him to give the terminal to me so he could tell me the code and I could enter it. I asked him: "What's the PIN?" "9-9-5-6," he answered. I entered it the terminal but it was still wrong. I asked him again: "What's your PIN?" "9-5-5-6," the new answer sounded. I entered it but the payment still didn't go through. I got irritated and yelled at the man: "JUST GIVE ME THE RIGHT PIN ALREADY!" He told me another combination: "9-9-6-5." I entered the numbers but it was still wrong. I had had enough and told the guy: "Fuck it, if you don't remember the right PIN, I'll take you right back to where I picked you up – to the taxi stand in Olari!"

I started to back up to turn the car around. Seeing that, the old man started to panic. He sobered up quite a bit and told me loud and clear: "No, it's 1-2-3-4!" I told him: "Come on, no one has a PIN like that, don't play stupid." I turned the car around to start driving to Olari. He looked scared and told me: "It is, 1-2-

3-4, I have that code!" I said: "Yeah, yeah, of course you do." "I really do," he kept confirming.

I stopped car and told him: "Okay, I will try one more time and if it isn't the right code, I will take you back to Olari!"

I entered the numbers and voila! The payment went through. It was the right PIN. The old man was just testing me, hoping to get home for free, without paying. The moment I told him I would take him back to Olari, he remembered the right PIN.

I got his money, he climbed out of the car and told me: "Wow, you're such a good person. I hope I'll meet you again." I said: "Yeah, I bet you will. Good night!"


## "Hey, we have a lady here with a bad back..."
## Bad back, my ass!

**July**. Night time on a workday. Unbelievable, how drunk could a Finnish woman be. It all happened at about 1am.

I was sitting at the taxi stand in **Kivenlahti, southwest Espoo**. A big bellied boy, who had consumed many many beers, approached the car from the yard of the nearby pubs. He had a request: "Could you drive to the yard of the pubs and pick up a woman who is a little bit drunk? Actually she has back problems and can't walk."

Big Boy entered the car and we drove for about 70 meters to get to the yard. There was a big blonde girl in her 40s, sitting on the ground. Another woman was standing next to her.

We exited the car with Big Boy and helped the blonde with the "tired" feet and back into the backseat of the car. I would say her legs were more "tired" than her back, because she couldn't get up at all. Okay, her back must have been hurting too. She couldn't stand up straight, because she would start grimacing from the pain.

I asked the woman where she was going. "Nearby, to …tie (about 1km)." She didn't tell me the number of the house, instead told me that she would guide me.

We arrived at an apartment building on the street. I thought we had arrived. The woman's sister, also blonde and wasted, helped her out of the car and escorted her to some stairs between two apartment houses. They were able to get to the lower apartments from there. I stayed in the car with Big Boy, to observe all of the action.

The blondes walked to the stairs and stopped. The one with the bad back sat down and said she isn't moving anywhere anymore. Her sister tried to tell her: "You can't stay outside all night. You have to come inside." The outside temperature was about 10 degrees Celsius.

I left the car and approached the women to see what to do next. I left the car on the street with its doors open, about 6-7 meters away from myself. I asked the tired blonde where she lived, which doorway was hers. She told me: "Right here," pointing right to the apartment building in front of us, to the middle doorway. There was about 30-35 meters to go. Then I asked: "Where are the keys to the house and the apartment?" "In my bag," was the tired answer.

We found the keys after looking in the bag for a few minutes. Then we thought how to get the woman to the doorway. The sister said: "Let's get going now." The tired blonde stood up, took two steps leaning on her sister and sat back down, saying: "No, I'm not going anywhere."

We took her between us with Big Boy and insisted to get going. No, she won't go, her back is hurting, the grown up patient kept moaning.

I offered Big Boy to lift the blonde up. She was against the idea at first. But we made a "chair" with our arms and took the blond down the stairs to the doorway. We made her stood up there, leaning against Big Boy.

A few moments later I realized that we could have gotten to the door by car if the tired blonde had told us. There was a way to her house from the end of the one next door.

Then the "sick" blonde remembered that her sister, who was on the stairs, had the keys. Now the sister was sitting and not moving. I told Big Boy: "I'm going to get the keys and return with the car." The car had its doors open in the middle of the street, all kinds of valuables just for the taking – 4 phones, money for change and the whole cash register.

I jogged back up the stairs to the car, grabbing the bag with the keys in it on the way.

I closed the car doors and drove around the house to the right door. The sister was also there by then. The sisters said their good byes to each other but the "tired" one still didn't enter the room. I had had enough and was too tired of the circus. I had given enough "humanitarian aid." I opened the door for the tired bird, held her under her arm and escorted her into the apartment. I told her: "Now you can sit for as long as you want to."

Then the rest of the party got back into the car. We drove to the Meripuisto hotel, about 500 meters away, where we parted our ways.

## Good dreams at the taxi stand predict raw shit on a shirt

**July**. Midnight on a weeknight. I had fallen asleep at the taxi stand in **Espoo center, Mid-Espoo**, when waiting for a client. I was just too tired of the "adventures" the last few nights. Finally an unknown colleague woke me up. I was just sipping sparkling wine in my dreams. Fuck, I was woken up at the best moment.

As soon as I had woken up, I got a fare to a local bar called Armadillo. I was so dizzy, I missed the right turn when driving there. On the next crossroads, where I could turn onto the highway, I realized I had made a little miscalculation.

I turned around and arrived at Armadillo. I picked up a girl, in her early twenties, wearing white pants and a white shirt and an older man, about 55-60 years old. I couldn't tell if they were a couple or what was going on. Anyway they were both wasted. The girl babbled a lot when she talked, I think she was missing a few teeth.

The "newly-weds" wanted to go to a McDonald's, which was a few kilometers away.

When we arrived, there were three cars in the line before us. The young lady came up with the "brilliant" idea to pause the meter until we were waiting. I paused it for a few minutes and when I saw that her attention was on the old man, I started it again. Win-win situation, as they say. We both got what we wanted.

After about 5 minutes she suddenly wanted to go take a leak. She didn't want to go to the bathroom in the McDonald's, but behind some bushes next to the building. To dry her "flower" after watering the grass, she asked for the old-man's shirt… She got it, exited the car and vanished into the darkness behind the bushes for 3-4 minutes. Now the half-naked old man exited the car. He waddled to the cashier window to investigate why the queue was moving so slowly. After he got an answer that told him nothing, he lit a cigarette to calm his nerves. At the same time the lady arrived with his T-shirt. Cinderella gave the old man his shirt and he put it on inside-out, leaving the shitty side out. Exactly, SHITTY. The lass returned with a shirt ruined with shit on one side.

She re-entered the car and sat on the back seat. The old man was still smoking outside.

It was our turn to get our food and I drove in front of the window. Miss Shitty started to repeat the cashier, what she had ordered, counting the various components. Finally I told the lady: "She knows what you ordered." Even the cashier started laughing.

The man paid the bill to the cashier and got in the car. He sat next to me, to the front seat. Fortunately he didn't ruin my seat with his shirt. The princess was already munching on her burger and fries, washing them down with some coke. She did it very loudly and unpleasantly like a big pig would devour its liquid grub.

We drove to a small neighborhood next to Espoo center. I think their friend lived there. During the drive the princess asked me if I would like some of her food. I politely refused. Just hearing how she mashed her food with her dirty, shitty fingers took all of my appetite.

We arrived at a yard of some row houses where there was a man waiting for the party – a friend of theirs looking like Karlsson. He was about 25-30 years old, looking like Big Mac himself – a big fat boy with stretched out sweat pants and a big shirt.

The old man paid the bill and we parted our ways. Finally. That fare gave me a trauma for quite a few days...

### You need the end the night with a hit against the tarmac

**August**. Weekend. I got a fare to a fun bar called M & H at midnight. It was in **Espoo center, Mid-Espoo**. Another bar with interesting clients where you could sometimes see people completely wasted during the middle of the day.

I was waiting right in front of the door. There was another vehicle in front of me, someone's private car.

First a giant came out of the bar – bald, wearing camouflage pants, tank boots and a leather jacket. He walked straight to my car, opened the rear door and walked back to the bar, about 6-7 meters. The bar door was opened again. A friend of the giant was escorted out between two men – he couldn't walk by himself. The two "extra wheels" who were holding him up, decided that their work was done and they could let the friend roam to the taxi by himself. They decided wrong.

First the giant's friend couldn't understand which car was the right one. He was beginning to lean towards the car in front of me on the first few steps. The giant noticed it and tried to pull him back. But his tires were so empty that when he was pulled, he just slammed to the ground, grazing the front of my car, like a big tree in the woods. Straight on the tarmac. The giant and an older gentleman went to investigate, how the Tree was doing and what condition was he in.

I also exited the car. I stopped next to the driver door. I was thinking to myself, what could be the consequences of a hit that hard. I was debating if I should approach them or what should I do.

I decided to not to anything at first. The giant and the old man tried to lift their friend up and asked me to help. I didn't like that idea. First of all, it isn't any of my business to help a fallen drunkard. Secondly, I have the right to carry clients who I consider adequate and polite. Third, I could tell that the giant and the old man could handle their friend themselves. And forth, they should have called the ambulance for the fallen tree, not a taxi. After all that analysis, I decided to sit back in the car.

I stayed observing the circus for a few moments. I saw that the fallen soldier couldn't get up and decided to leave. I knew that if I picked up the trio, I would have a big adventure on my hands, which wouldn't be worth the money.

I exited once more, closed the rear door, sat back in the car and drove off.

### That same night. The big lady who also liked to lie down on the tarmac

**August**. Weekend. On the same night that a very drunk gentleman "kissed" the ground in front of a bar in **Espoo center**, I got a call to the local **IKEA shopping center**.

I drove to the end of the street where I was stopped by a fence that surrounded the area. I waited for a few minutes but nobody showed up. I called the customer's phone and said I had arrived and explained where I was exactly. As it turned out, I was waiting in the wrong place. I drove back to the other end of the street, the drunk lady giving me directions. I saw a big round body waving at me in a dark parking lot. Okay, I was in the right place.

I picked up the drunk lady, who weighed about 120-130 kilograms and we drove to her apartment, about 3 kilometers away. She had a plastic bag containing drinks and food. It was almost 2 am. I don't know where she got them. Anyway she wanted to go to her apartment. She wanted to pick up her poodle (that's what she told me) and a couple of bottles of vodka. Then she wanted to go some woods in **Nuuksio**[68], where her summer house supposedly was.

Okay. We were driving to her apartment. On the way we went around some curves and she kept leaning on my right arm. It isn't exactly pleasant when a girl weighing about 130 kilograms is pressing on your hand. Not exactly exciting.

We arrived at her house and drove to the last doorway. It was almost dark. The only light was coming from the doorway. There was a bit of sidewalk to the right of the car and some bushes, about 3 meters high. She said that she would leave her bag, go to her apartment and pick up her vodka and her dog. "Okay. I'll wait," I promised her.

She then tried to exit the car in that dark and narrow spot. It wasn't the easiest. She pulled herself up

---

[68]*Nuuksio* – *a national park in northwest Espoo. It is located 40 kilometers to the northwest of Helsinki.*

on the open car door. She then faced the car, stepped a bit to the left, closed the door and right away slid to the ground, clipping the car's side.

I exited to see if she was all right and to help her up. But she had gotten up mysteriously fast. Only her shoe was lost. I aimed my flashlight into the darkness, and on the grass we found Cinderella's slipper. Then she started to totter towards the doorway, asking me to join her. I refused politely and added that I would wait in the car.

I waited for 5-6 minutes. She arrived with a mutt the size of the Baskerville hound[69] in one hand and a plastic bag with two one-liter vodka bottles in the other.

I exited the car again to open the trunk so that the dog could get in. I asked Cinderella: "So THIS is the little poodle, huh?" "Well, it's a little dog, isn't it. He won't bite. He's friendly," she said of her horse-sized dog…

We started to drive towards the summer house. The roads in **northern Espoo** are traditionally full of turns, so the lady leaned on my arm with her body every time we turned right. The dog didn't like the

---

[69] „The hound of the baskervilles" – *a story by Arthur Conan Doyle, which contain the characters of detective Sherlock Holmes and doctor Watson.*

roads either – it was under stress and flapping around in the back, trying to find the right position to survive the trip. At one moment he was lying down and then sat again. He tried to stand up but then realized that the car was too small and sat or lay down again. Finally he got in a position so that he was sitting up and stared at the road in front of us with his giant head. The view of the dark trunk and the colossal head looked pretty scary from the rear view mirror.

After driving for about 10 minutes we arrived at the lady's two-floor summer house. It seemed to be a safe atmosphere because the house's door was completely open. She paid the bill without any problems after which I helped her lift her stuff out of the car, along with the dog. After all of that she thanked me for suffering through the trip with her. Well it wasn't the worst fare in the world. On the contrary, it was pretty interesting.

### From the nursing home to buy some vodka with an old man

**September**. Monday night. **southwest Espoo**. I got a call from a nursing home. I picked up a totally wasted 65 year-old man who wanted to go to a shopping center in **Espoonlahti** (about 2km) to buy some vodka.

I took him to the center in Espoonlahti. I stayed outside, waiting in the car until he returned with his vodka.

He calmly got back in the car and we drove back to the nursing home.

*9. A tired Sunday shopper in the shopping center in Espoonlahti.*

When we arrived, he turned out to be so wasted that he didn't understand the concept of money when he was trying to pay the bill. First he offered me a tenner but the bill was bigger. The old man thought the tenner was a 50-euro bill. Finally I managed to convince him that it indeed was a tenner. Then he found his 50-euro bill and thought it was a tenner, so he offered me that in addition to the first tenner.

After a while, we managed to pay the bill. When he exited the car, he couldn't understand which way was his home – the nursing home. He started to stride away from it. I pulled his sleeve and escorted him to the door where there was an angry nurse already waiting for him. I wonder if the old man got a taste of the vodka or if they took it right away.

## Getting some food with a yelling couple from the barbecue

**September**. Friday evening. It was about 6 pm. I was at the taxi stand in **Kivenlahti, southwest Espoo**. I saw a couple, about 40-50 years old, approaching from a line of pubs. The man looked like Jesus – long gray hair combed apart from the middle of his head, although his body type was more oval-like. He was wearing shorts and a T-shirt. He was so wasted, he would have definitely fallen if he hadn't been leaning on the woman.

The couple got to the car and took a seat. The old man said: "Let's go to … Grill (about 300 meters from the taxi stand)." Then the woman started moaning about something to him. He barked to her: "Shut up, shut up!" She kept quiet for a few minutes until we arrived at the barbecue. She started nagging again: "You won't get food, you won't bring any food into the car!" I tried to calm the situation and told them: "You can bring it in the car if you don't spill anything on the seats or on the floor."

The old man went to get his food, which the woman still didn't agree with. She exited the car and said some pretty harsh words to the old man in front of the counter. The she returned to the car and asked me: "Are you having a bad day? Do you not like it here in **Finland**?" Like I had a problem with the purchase or with the old man. I told her: "It depends on the customers I have." She kept moaning: "My life isn't easy either. I have to work every day too." "So? Why are you telling me," I couldn't understand.

In the meantime, the old man had gotten his kebab and fries. He started approaching the car with them. The woman jumped out of the car again like a mother lion, yelling to the old man: "You are not coming in the car with that food!" He still didn't agree with the lady, and started arguing with her, walking to the car at the same time. The bird stepped in front of the man and screamed at him: "I decide who gets in the car and who doesn't!" He indifferently pushed her to the side and sat in the front seat next to me.

Then the woman entered the car and was quiet for a moment. I asked "Where are you going by the way?" "**Laurinlahti** (about 1.5km)," was the answer from the back. I asked her: "Where exactly in Laurinlahti?" "Laurinlahti," was the answer again. The old man calmly told me the exact address and we got on our way.

When we arrived, the woman quickly exited and started walking towards the house. The old man stayed inside to pay the bill. It was about 18 euros. He gave me a 50-euro bill. I didn't have change and told him: "I would need to give you all of my change," and asked: "Do you have anything smaller?" "No I don't. Just give me back 25," the calmness himself answered. I gave him back the money and we parted our ways. I was wondering how could he be calm enough to put up with the constant yelling.


### The drunk woman lost in the uproar of her hormones

**September**. It was about 5 am. I got a fare in **Saunalahti**, next to **Kivenlahti, southwest Espoo**.

When I arrived I called the customer and said: "Hello, you have ordered a taxi. Do you still want it?" The call was answered by a drunk woman. She listened to my monologue but didn't say anything. I just heard how she told somebody: "I don't know, I don't understand who is calling me."

I waited for a few seconds hoping someone would speak to me, but nothing. I repeated what I said, this time a bit louder: "You have ordered a taxi, do you still want it?" Then I heard her mumble something to me: "Y-y-yes, I w-want it." So I continued: "Okay, I'm right in front of your house waiting for you." Then I heard an order: "Turn around and turn left!" I thought: "What?! Where do I have to turn?" Then I thought maybe the customer already sees me from somewhere.

I backed up and turned on the street. I saw a drunk woman talking to the phone sitting on the sidewalk to the right of me. There was a man next to her, barely able to stand up.

I drove next to them. I stopped and waited for them to get in the car.

The woman got up from the sidewalk and tottered to the car and approached my door. She started a conversation through the window: "Hey, could you wait for 5 minutes?" "Yes, I can," I answered. She asked: "How much would it cost?" "Well about 4 euros," I told her. She thought about it for a moment and then said: "Okay, wait here. Or actually, could you come back later?" I told her: "No I can't. I'm waiting right here." "Okay, wait here then," she agreed. She went back to the guy and started making out with him right on the street.

I was waiting about 4-5 meters away from them. I heard some of the conversation, when the woman said: "I know you want me, but..." "Damn it, just decide who wants who or what," I thought to myself sitting in the car.

Finally, after about 4 minutes she approached the car. She asked: "Hey, how much is the bill?" I told her: "12 euros." "Okay, I'll pay the bill," she answered and added: "I'm not coming right now. I'll come later. Can you return later to pick me up?" I told her: "I don't know where I'll be later – maybe in Helsinki, maybe in Vantaa." "Okay, I'll pay the bill," she told me. Then she started again: "But can you pick me up later?" I repeated myself and emphasized: "I DON'T KNOW WHERE I WILL BE LATER. IT'S A BUSY DAY. I could be very far from here. There will be another taxi. Just order one again." "Oh, okay," she finally understood.

She started to give me her card to pay the bill but it slipped out of her hand and fell in the car. She started panicking: "Oh my god! What now?!" I calmly told her: "Nothing. See, here's your card," and put the card in the terminal.

She paid the bill and I headed back to Kivenlahti. While I was turning the car around, the woman had sat back down on the sidewalk and the man had decided to take a leak 4-5 meters away from her.

Looking at the picture I just thought – what a cute, romantic couple. This will be a happy marriage for years...

### The "jackpot" from Kalaonnentie

**September**. Friday. It was daytime, even before noon. I got a fare from **Kalaonnentie**[70] in **Matinkylä, southern Espoo**. I didn't feel especially lucky when I got there and saw who was waiting for me.

The call had come from a medical institution. There was a woman, about 50-55 years old, sitting in the parking lot. She was shivering all over her body. She had two sticks next to her on one side and a backpack on the other side. She had a sneaker on one foot and a black boot on the other.

---

[70]***Kalaonnetie** – Fishluckstreet in Finnish*

She couldn't get up by herself. So I helped her and escorted her to the front seat. I couldn't figure out if she was ill or did she have a bad hangover.

I asked where she was headed. "To the health center in Tapiola," she answered with a shaking voice. She then asked me: "Is there an ATM somewhere?" She needed cash. I told her she could pay by card. She told me she could but she still needed cash. I told her I didn't know where an ATM would be, that maybe we could find one in Tapiola. In Finland, ATMs are like sunny days in Estonia – there aren't many.

We were passing a gas station near Matinkylä. We had to go on the highway to get to **Tapiola**.

Suddenly she said: "Let's stop here! I want to buy cigarettes." I pulled into the parking lot of the gas station, stopped in front of the store and waited for her to get her smokes. Instead she asked me: "Can you get cash from here?" I told her she couldn't: "You can buy your cigarettes here if you want to." "Well, I need to get some cash first," she kept making things difficult. Damn it! I told her: "You can use your card to pay for the smokes!" "No-no, I need cash first." "For fuck's sake. You even don't know what you want," I thought to myself.

So we drove to Tapiola. I asked if she knew where an ATM could be there. "I don't know. I'm sure there's one somewhere," she answered. She added: "Actually, I can go to the ATM after I go to the health center and then buy some cigarettes. It's not that important right now." What the hell?! Is talking bullshit their national disease, I thought.

When we were about 500 meters from the destination, we arrived at a busy intersection. One driver had stopped in the middle of the crossroads so there was a traffic jam.

So I stopped and the woman started moaning: "Why are we stopping?! Keep going!" I asked: "Where to? You can see that there are cars in the way!" "Well, just keep going." She didn't make sense.

I just said nothing and quietly waited for the street to clear.

We arrived at the health center and the crazy woman and I went our separate ways.

**Unforgettable shift. Stepping on the same rake twice. Unavoidable**
**October**. The daily shift had started promisingly. I got my Hyundai from the **Suomenoja** dealership in

**southern Espoo** at about half past five. The Korean "harvester" had gotten its service done during the day. I started my shift and got the first fare to the **Olari** district nearby.

I drove to the right spot. I saw a skinny man, about 160-165cm tall, about 45 years old, in front of the house. He was shivering, leaning on the house with one hand. He had on a gray work jacket with lots of pockets. He was wearing a cap and gray baggy pants that looked like pajamas. For the set to be perfect, the look on his face was completely glazed, like a fish.

I opened the door from the inside and saw that he had a walking disability. He was dragging his feet about 5 centimeters at a time. He moved slowly and steadily to the car and slid to the front seat.

"Where to," I asked. "To Olari K...," he told me. Okay, let's go. Olari K... is one of those "pubs" where "tired" people go to have their warm beer and socialize.

We got there without any trouble. I stopped the car in front of the pub windows. I drove on for about 1.5 meters so the customer wouldn't have to go through one door to another. He didn't agree, though.

I waited for the guy to look for his money and pay the bill but he wasn't moving. I asked: "What is it? Is there a problem?" "This isn't the place," he said importantly. I told him: "Yes it is!" "No it's not," he kept arguing. "It's not the right door! This is the hair salon's door. The right door is right there," he said. "Oh, I'm sorry I drove past it," I answered ironically and added: "I'll back up 2 meters so you'd be happy."

I backed up and the king was pleased. He paid the bill, which was about 8 euros. Then he exited the car and dragged himself in the bar. I didn't know I would see the same man again, only in a different condition.

## The same night. The same clown – the same rake

At night, at about 1 am, I was looking for one more fare before I ended my shift and I got one, it was unforgettable.

On the way to **Olari** center in **southern Espoo**, I got a fare to the same pub – Olari K… The same place I had been at the start of the shift. I looked at the order and saw that the customer was paying with a **city card**[71]. I thought maybe it was the same guy I had taken there at 6 pm. He also paid his bill with a

---

[71] ***The co-pay*** – *many "city cards" have a certain sum the customer has to pay himself. Some cards don't have it, so the co-pay is 0 euros.*

city card. Then I doubted it – nobody could sit in the same bar for 7 hours and just drink.

Before I arrived, the dispatcher warned me that a couple of taxis had been to the bar but refused to pick up the customer because of some problem. "Okay, got it. I'll go and have a look," I told them.

When I arrived, I saw that same guy, who I had brought there, sitting in front of the pub door (there was a small room before you entered the bar). He was wasted and still shivering.

I approached him and told him to get up, that the taxi had arrived to take him home. His movement was uncoordinated and he still didn't get up. I grabbed him from under his arm and pulled him up. At the same time, the Arab owner or manager of the bar came. He picked up the drunk character and brought him to my car and sat him down on the front seat. The manager asked me: "Do you know where this clown is going?" I answered: "Actually I do, I brought him here." "Okay, got it," he told me and that was it.

We arrived at his house. He gave me his city card to pay the bill. I slid it through the terminal. Everything worked. He started to pay the excess part, which was 2.80 but couldn't get his wallet from his pocket. I told him: "Wait, I'll take it myself!" I got the wallet and took a handful of cents from it. I put the wallet back in his pocket and told him what was going to happen: "Good. The bill has been paid. Let's go now, I'll help you in the house so you wouldn't freeze outside."

I opened his seatbelt, exited the car and opened his door. I grabbed his arms and pulled him out of the car.

We slowly started moving towards the house. Suddenly, one of his legs wasn't able to support him and he fell on his side. I picked him up and just dragged him to the door, holding him from underneath his arm. He couldn't walk right before he went to the bar, after going the bar he didn't know what the hell walking was.

Then the circus started. As he couldn't stand up by himself, I had to hold him up. I was still holding him from under his arm and I put his other hand on the door, so he would have some support. I asked: "Where are your keys?" "In my pocket," he told me. "Which one?" I tried to get more precise information about the keys, because there were about 12 pockets just on his jacket. He tried to find the keys, his movement was as slow as a snail. I waited for about a minute and asked: "Can you find your keys or not?" I saw that I could search for them faster – I started going through his pockets to get him inside faster. I didn't dare to leave him outside – he would have frozen before morning. The temperature was close to 0 degrees.

He had everything but the keys in his pockets – a lighter, wallet, pack of cigarettes, phone, etc. Half his fortune was there. I told him: "You don't have any keys. What am I supposed to do with you?! Where should I take you now?!" He didn't have any ideas.

I contacted the dispatcher to get some help with the situation. The woman who answered ignorantly told me: "No, I don't know!" "Why the fuck are you sitting there if you don't know anything?!" I got angry at the unhelpful fool.

I tried to get some help from the clown and asked him: "Hey, do you maybe have some friends or family nearby? I could take you there?" "U-u-umm," he just said. "Yeah, I have some in Kuunkatu street, Olari," he said, finally able to put together a sentence. I told him to call the friend. He did, but the phone was switched off and we couldn't reach him.

I tried the dispatcher again: "Seriously, what am I supposed to do with him, where should I take him?" Fortunately a different person answered that time. She recommended: "Call the locksmith service, they can open the door." "Okay, good point, thanks." I praised the Kitty for the bright idea.

During my call I let go of the clown's arm. He slid down on the door like thick spit. I pulled him back up again and helped him hold on to the door handle. I told him to call the company that serviced the doors. He tried, he really did. But what can you accomplish when you have been sipping alcohol for the last 7 hours? Of course he was having trouble getting his phone and it was even more difficult to enter the right number on his virtual keyboard.

I had had enough. The door maintenance number was on the wall. I called them myself and explained the situation to the technician and asked him to get there with the keys.

Then I dragged the clown back to the car and sat him down again until the technician would get there. I got in too. Then he asked me: "Why the hell are we sitting here?" Fuck! He couldn't understand anything. I explained: "We are waiting for the door maintenance! Otherwise you can't get in! You don't have your keys and nowhere else to go. I can't leave you outside, it's only 3 degrees." "They should be in my pocket," the smart ass told me. I tried again: "You don't have your keys. You looked for them, I looked for them. We went through all your pockets. You don't have them!" "Well, when I left home, I had them with me," the poor clown tried to explain. "No biggie, I'll start the meter again and you'll pay for the time we're pleasantly spending together here." He looked at the meter and was quiet.

I went outside to have a cigarette. When I finished and got back in, he had already slumped. He had fallen asleep with his head on his chest. I feared he would piss his pants or puke in the car. That kind of shit happens sometimes.

I waited for about 5 minutes and had another smoke. The technician was nowhere to be seen. I sat back in the car and was there for about 15 minutes before having a third cigarette. He still hadn't arrived. When I had been waiting for half an hour, I called the maintenance number again. I inquired about Mr. Opener. "He is already on his way," they gave me hope.

After about 5 more minutes, a white van appeared with Mr. Opener. I asked how far was he coming from that he took so long. The old man said: "From nearby. I had a call 15 minutes ago and had to take that first." "Got it," I told him and waited for him to open the door. Before doing that he approached the clown sleeping in my car. We woke him up and Mr. Opener handed him a receipt to sign. He thought about 10 seconds what his name was and then signed it.

We left the tired fellow in the car and went to see how we could open the door and where the clown's apartment was. It turned out that it was on the third floor, so we had to drag him up there.

We went back to the car with the technician. We dragged the clown out of the car to get him upstairs. Yeah – we were clearly too optimistic. The drunkard managed to drag himself to the door but then his strength ended – he fell down like an empty bag. Our only choice was to pick him up. The technician grabbed him from his arms, I took his legs and we went up the stairs to the third floor. We placed the clown in his bed.

Then I took off, I had had enough of the circus. Mr. Opener stayed to close the doors. The next morning the clown must have had a great morning – a crazy hangover and a 90-euro bill for the taxi drive and for the door.

*"Why the fuck are you calling me in the morning?!"*

**October**. Early morning, it was about 5 am. I had just dropped a customer off and got a fare to **Raastala**, the district next to the one I was in. It's a small neighborhood in **eastern Espoo**, near **Leppävaara**.

I stopped in front of the right house. All the windows were dark. I called the customer. The phone was answered by a very drunk and sleepy old man. I asked: "Did you order a taxi?" The response was filled with disgusting language: "What?! I haven't ordered anything! Why the fuck are you fucking calling me so early in the morning? Dick!" "Okay, got it," I told him. I ended the call and said out loud: "Go fuck yourself too!" I had gotten another empty order. It happens, especially on the weekend. Along with the juicy verbal garnish.

*"How many times do I have to tell you before you understand?!"*

A night in **October**. It was about 2 am. I had just dropped off some "tough guys" in **Espoo center**, **Mid-Espoo**. They promised to drive to Helsinki, but actually drove for only 1.5 kilometers to their house. I wasn't in the best mood.

Right away, I got my next fare from a fine "kiosk-pub" called M&H, which was nearby. If you want adventures, go to Espoo center during the night – you're bound to get an experience and ruin your nerves.

Another clown came from the pub: "Hey, take me to another place, better than this, which would still be open." I told him: "There is nothing open in **Espoo**. If anything, there's the Kannunkulma open nearby, if you want to go." "No-no, Kannunkulma is closed," the wise ass started arguing. I tried explaining: "No it's not, I just came from there with some customers. I know it's open until 2:30." "No-no-no, I'm not going there, it's closed," the clown kept arguing. I repeated myself: "No it's not, I was JUST there." "No-no," he still refused to believe me and added: "We'll go somewhere else, to a place which is still open!" I told the imbecile again: "All the places close at 2am! There is nowhere to go in Espoo after 2! There might be a bar open until 4 in **Helsinki**!!" I had to repeat myself multiple times. The fucking clown was so wasted that he was practically lying down on the back seat but he still wanted to go to a bar and kept arguing.

Then the chump started talking, being half asleep: "Well, let's go to Helsinki then." I asked him: "Where do you want to go in Helsinki?" "Well I don't know. What's still open?" he kept inquiring. I told him: "The Milli Club might be open until the morning. Do you want to go there?" "Well okay, take me there," he said, the fool finally making up his mind.

On the **Turunväylä** highway, right before **Leppävaara**, he started insisting: "I need to go to the bank." I explained to him: "There aren't any banks on the highway at 2 am. When we get to Helsinki, you can go to the ATM there!" It's not like there's a gas station or an ATM after every 100 meters.

Like that wasn't enough, before the exit to Leppävaara he started asking: "Where are we going anyway?" I told him: "You wanted to go to the Milli Club in Helsinki and an ATM before that! Have you changed your mind?" "Umm, oh, well I don't know," he mumbled. I told him to make up his mind: "Think fast, are you going to Helsinki or to Leppävaara! We are approaching the exit!" "Well, let's go to Leppävaara then," the fool finally decided.

When I was turning on to the exit, doing about 100km/h, he got an idea to shake my hand, I think. He started patting my shoulder and pulling my right arm. I got angry and yelled: "Don't touch me! Do you want to get us in an accident?"

Well, I guess he didn't understand shit, he was so intoxicated.

After a few minutes, we arrived at the Sello shopping center, next to the Leppävaara train station. A night club is also located there. The ATM is right next to the club's door.

I stopped there and the imbecile started asking again: "Hey, which places are still open?" I explained for the fifth time: "THERE ARE NO PLACES OPEN IN ESPOO! THERE MIGHT BE SOME BARS OPEN IN HELSINKI!" Fuck, how many times can you explain the same thing to a person that should have a brain? "Well, let's go to Helsinki," the idiot started selling his "business plan" to me. I told him: "You just wanted to go there and then you wanted to go here! Now we're here and I'm not taking you to Helsinki. Actually, I'm not going anywhere with you! Go take some cash from the ATM! Pay the bill and then you stay here! See, there's a kebab place right here, you can eat there!" "No, I don't want to eat, I don't want to eat," he said, refusing my proposals. "You can take another taxi for all I care. I'm not taking you anywhere," I said, trying to make the situation clear to him.

He didn't go to the ATM, he found some money in his pockets, 35 euros. He explained: "I don't have any more money." The bill was about 26 euros. I told him: "Just give me 25 and we're even. Now leave!" "Hey, do you have a lighter?" He still didn't understand me. I told him I had one and gave him my malfunctioning lighter. "You're such a cool guy, you're such a cool guy," he mumbled and wanted to light his cigarette in the car. I yelled again: "You aren't smoking in the car, otherwise you'll get fined!" Then I added once AGAIN: "Get out of the car!" Finally I got rid of him and drove away.

No wonder I smoked half a pack of smokes during my shifts, if I had to deal with these kinds of people.

### Another typical "nerve tester"

**October**. **Matinkylä** taxi stand in **southern Espoo**. The taxi stand was temporarily moved next to a local bar.

At 2 am a drunk old man, in his sixties, waved to me in front of the bar, so I would drive to him. He just couldn't walk the 10 meters – he was such a VIP, the car had to come to him.

I picked up the "handicapped" man and asked: "Where are we going?" "To **Suurpelto**[72]," he answered. It is a district of apartment buildings behind Olari, about 9 kilometers north of Matinkylä. I asked, to specify: "To Piilipuuntie (there are 3 bigger streets in the district and the fares usually start or end from that street)?" "Yes," he answered in an exhausted tone.

So we got to Suurpelto, I turned to Piilipuuntie and asked him: "Which one is your house? Where should I stop?" I think he had fallen asleep, he opened his eyes, looked around for a moment and arrogantly asked: "Wait, where the hell are you driving anyway?!" I told him: "You wanted to go to Piilipuuntie!" "No-no-no," was the answer. "To …tie," the old man with the walking "disability" said. I explained to him: "I asked you if you're going to Piilipuuntie and you told me that you were!" He then calmed down a bit and apologized: "Oh, sorry, I meant the other street."

I turned the car around and stopped about 100 meters later in front of a house. Then the old man started looking for his money. He searched through his pockets for about 3-4 minutes and asked me:

---

[72]***Suurpelto*** *– A new district next to Kehä II, between Hentta, Mankkaa and Olari districts.*

"Hey, am I drunk?" I told him: "Yes you are, now pay the bill!" The brainless fellow then asked: "Where is my wallet?" "How should I know, where YOUR wallet is. Find the money and get out of the car!" All the theatrics had annoyed me. I explained: "You had the whole way to look for your wallet and your money. Stop acting stupid and find your damn wallet!"

The "handicapped" old man was moving like a gymnast on the back seat to find the money in his pockets.

Finally I had had enough and told him: "Do you have the money or should I take you back to where I picked you up?!" Then he got startled: "Whoa, whoa, wait, I'll find it right away!" And voila! He found his wallet right away. Another ape was trying to test my nerves, to find out what I was going to do if he didn't pay the bill. Damn it, a full grown man but pulling stunts like that.

### It isn't easy to walk on a cobblestoned street on high heels and drunk as hell

**October**. I picked up a familiar woman from a pub in **Soukka, southwest Espoo**. I had driven her before.

When she got out of the entertainment establishment with her high heels, stepping on the cobblestoned street, she lost her balance and almost fell on her stomach. Fortunately the side of my car came first, so she collided with it first. Then she tried really hard to open the rear door as she was hanging on the door handle. When she managed to open it, she just fell in the car with her feet still hanging out of the door. After half a minute she got her tired legs in the car. The destination was about 8 kilometers away, an apartment building.

When we arrived, she paid the bill and apologized: "Sorry, I'm too drunk. It's my birthday today." "Congratulations," I said.

Despite being really drunk, she knew exactly where to go and didn't cause any problems. People can act normal if they just try.


### The two flat turtles
**October**. It was about 2 am. I picked up two completely wasted female turtles from a "popular" bar in **Matinkylä, southern Espoo**. One flatter than the other. They were lucky to notice the taxi.

One of them wanted to walk home but the other one didn't allow it. They argued about it until we arrived at the house of one turtle.

I asked: "Where are the ladies going?" They told me they were going to **Kala-Matti**, which was about a kilometer from the bar. I accidentally got the addresses mixed up and turned to the one-way street **of Kala-Maija**. Of course I didn't bother to turn around again because the woman, who was a bit more sober than the other, convinced me to keep going. She told me: "You can go through here!" "Well okay," I responded shortly, although I didn't know if there was a way through there, which was acceptable for a car.

So we were driving through a yard on a sidewalk. It got really narrow at one point. There was a high bush left of us and a stone wall, about 1,5 meters high, to the right of us. We barely made it through. I heard the bush "drawing flames" on the car when I was driving through there.

We finally made it to the "cave" of the more crooked turtle. She started arguing that it wasn't her house. After some time, we forced her out of the car. Her friend was yelling at her: "Why are you arguing?! You're so wasted, you don't know where you are!"

We headed to a street nearby with the other "injured bride." She kept teaching me: "Go straight, go straight." I told her: "I know where the street is." But when we got to her house she wasn't able to tell me to stop. I drove past the entry to the yard, for about 15 meters. She started yelling: "You drove past the right place. Don't you know where the house is?!" I calmly told her: "Well I really don't." At the same time I was thinking to myself: "Damn it, it's dark outside and there's some shit falling from the sky. You can't see any numbers on the houses. And I can't know every alcoholic turtles shed in Espoo, can I?"

I backed up for about 10 meters, after which she somehow agreed to pay the bill and exit the car. Of course that took another 5 minutes because finding her wallet was a difficult process. And finding money from the wallet was even harder. Finally she found her card but she didn't give it to me. Instead she started asking: "Is it raining outside?" I told her: "Yes, give me the card now!"

I got the card and gave it back to her along with the terminal, so she could enter her PIN. But she was still worried: "Is it really raining? Is it raining heavily?" I said: "No, it's just a drizzle. Just enter your PIN!" I couldn't take it! How much time do you need to pay your bill?! Do you ask cashiers in stores if it's raining outside and how heavily is it raining?! And several times.

Finally she managed to enter her PIN and pay her bill. When she left the car, she forgot her dirty plastic bag on the floor of the car. I yelled at her: "Hey, you left your bag! I don't need it!" The turtle took her bag, looking at me with her glazed eyes, thanked me and started walking to her cave. And that's what it's like every night, was all I could think.


## "Come help me put the heater on my car!"

**November**. Weekend. At about 2 am, another dick managed to piss me right off.

I got a fare in **Kauniainen**, a small neighbor town of **Espoo**. There was about 8 minutes to drive. A long way to go, but I decided to take the fare. You could get some decent and polite customers at that time on weekends. I was hoping that maybe a family wanted to go home with their kids, which is often the case in the area. People visit each other and sometimes stay for too long.

I managed to get to the right place through the narrow slippery streets. I turned into a parking lot and started looking for the customer.

An old man, in his sixties, appeared from between some cars, totally wasted. He was approaching my car, wearing a white sweater and some pants from the seventies. I waited for him to get in but instead he approached my window. I rolled it down and asked: "What's the problem?" The man explained: "Heyyy, come help me set the preheater timer for my car." The kind that you can connect to a post in the parking lot, so the car would be warm in the morning.

I took my flashlight and we managed to set the timer. The clown was happy. I forgot to start the meter so the first 5 minutes were free to the old man.

After locking his car doors, he entered the car. I asked: "Where are we headed?" "Oh, nearby, to my friend's place," he said.

We drove for about 400-500 meters. I was swearing to myself: "Did I really drive for 5 kilometers to help a drunkard set his car heater and then drive him for 500 meters to a friend's house?"

We arrived at the destination. I entered a tip of 3.60 on the meter, just to get something for my trouble.

For fuck's sake! He gave me the city card. I was swearing to myself again. Fuck, you're paying with the city's money just to go drinking at a friend's house. What a patriot!

He gave me a fiver to pay the excess part, which was 2.80 euros. I thought he would leave me the 2.20 as a tip. I didn't even start to look for the change and hoped that he would get out of the car. But no! The old man stared at me and asked: "Aren't you giving my change back?" I got angry and told him: "Fuck, I just wasted 15 minutes to get here from Kauniaise, deal with your heater and now you're asking for your 2 euros?" "Well, I bet you're going to have a good night, you'll get your money," he told me. I told him: "It's none of your business, how much money I get or don't get. You should pay for me helping you!" Then he started looking for coins from his pockets. When I saw that I said: "Come on, let it be, just leave!" He left the car and I drove away, looking for the next customer, hopeful that it would be a better one.

## The same night. The old lady in a coma who could drink but not walk

**November**. **Olari, southern Espoo**. It was about 1 am. A totally wasted old lady, about 65 years old, appeared, on two walking sticks, barely able to stand up. She had a pink and black backpack on her. She was in a complete "traffic jam". I wasted about 5 minutes, just to "pack" her into the car.

We drove to an apartment building next to **Matinkylä** (about 3.5 kilometers). She gave me her city card during the drive, coughing and clearing her throat at the same time. I thought I would add a "helping tax" (it's a possibility with some cards) for helping another clown.

I wanted to add 4.50 but accidentally entered the wrong code on the meter and it added 15.40. Shit, whatever! It was a decent cost for the shit I had been through. I didn't make a big deal of my mistake.

When we arrived at her house, the same process that had happened at the start of the drive, repeated. I opened the door for her, helped her up, gave her the sticks and helped her to her door so she wouldn't fall down. Then she asked me to unlock her door. There you go. At your service!

I managed to get her inside without any further adventure and left to get another customer.

### Old love does not rust

**November**. During the same night, when I had been regulated a pensioners preheater in **Espoo center**, I drove to **Kivenlahti, southwest Espoo** after that. I got another "fun" fare there – to a pub in **Latokaski** – a small district between Espoo center and **Espoonlahti**. About 80% of the customers coming from there are "aliens" who are lost and don't know where their home is.

I drove there for about 8-9 minutes. There was a couple waiting for me in front of the bar – a man and a woman, both about 65 years old, both utterly wasted.

They got in the car and I heard right away how the woman started moaning at the old man: "Why the hell did you call a taxi? We only have 500 meters to go!" The old man yelled at the woman: "Damn it, I'm so drunk, I can't walk!" She didn't let up though: "I don't have any money to pay for the taxi!" The man answered: "Neither do I!" To hell with it! Try to drive around with these kinds of imbeciles – you're going to be at the same level in the morning.

We arrived at the old couple's parking lot. The woman got out of the car as soon as I had stopped. The man saw that and yelled: "Hey, come back! I don't have any money!" The woman yelled something and kept going towards their house. The man realized that he wouldn't be helped by her lady and that he would have to pay the bill.

He searched for his card and paid the bill, which was 9.80. Nine euros was the starting cost.

After paying the bill, he still didn't want to follow his great love. He tried to start a conversation with me, asking a very common question: "Where are you from?" "**Estonia**," I tiredly answered. "Yes, yes, Estonia is a good country. **Finland** is a great country too, isn't it," he was looking for my approval. "Yeah, yeah, just go now," I told him. Then I explained: "I've got another fare coming up and I have to pick up a customer…" Hearing that, he finally decided to leave the car and I could drive away.

## The hippo family from Leppävaara

**December**. Evening on a weekend. I got a fare to **Leppävaara** district, in **eastern Espoo**, on the border of **Espoo** and **Helsinki**. When I arrived to the place where the taxi had been ordered from, it turned out that a drunk family of hippos had been let loose from the zoo. The company was made up of four people, all in their fifties, all overweight, all wasted. Three of them were male, one was female. They all looked like blown up Michelin men. I was lucky to be driving the big Hyundai. The Merc would have stretched out under all that weight.

So the local circus got in the car and I waited for some information so I would know where to go. But it seemed that it wasn't important at all for them.

Right away they started yelling and screaming – hahaha, blablabla. I calmed them down and asked for their attention, to get some info about where the circus was headed. "Well, let's go to Blue Ray." It was a local bar, about 1.5 kilometers away.

The screaming and yelling continued. Everybody had something to say. Everyone was talking over each other, one topic nastier than the other. I didn't even want to listen. I was thinking, what a great party. They drove 2 kilometers but acted like they were driving 200.

Fortunately the trip really was just 2 kilometers. I got rid of them in front of the bar and the hippo in the front seat even left me a tip of 2.40. Thanks for compensating for the emotional trauma!

## The travelling oldsters

**December.** Nighttime on a weekend. I got a "fun" party to travel with from **southeast Espoo**.

I was sitting at the taxi stand in **Tapiola** and an old lady approached the car, about 70 years old. She got in the car and said: "Let's find my man – he should be wandering around in Tapiola with his friends." At a bus stop about 100 meters from the taxi stand, the woman noticed three blokes . I think they were discussing some important matters because they were using their arms to make their point.

I stopped the car and picked the trio up. We drove for about 1.5 kilometers to the McDonald's in **Niittykumppu**.

We dropped off two of the fellows at an apartment building and headed back to Tapiola with the couple.

When we arrived, the man made a colorful gesture – took out his big wallet, spat on his fingers and pulled out 20 euros. He pushed the bill to my hand and told me: "Keep the change." I thanked him for the "spiced up" money. The bill itself was about 18 euros.

I helped the man out of the car and drove off. Then I noticed that he had ruined the front seat with his boots. It looked like a dirty pig had rolled around there.

Maybe he gave me the tip so I could clean the car and wouldn't be so angry…

### The flying Finn from Westend

**December**. I got a fare from a private house in **Tapiola, southeast Espoo**. I drove to the address. I saw a big, beautiful villa, with an expensive SUV in front of it.

I had been waiting for about a minute in front of the gate, when suddenly a person appeared from the darkness. He slowed down for a bit and stopped. Mr. Comet decided to wave at the house. I'm not sure he could see anyone there. Then he approached my car.

When he came through the gate, he didn't slow down, he just banged against the rear door of the car. Then I realized that he wasn't in the best condition.

He was about 40 years old. He got in the car with a bang similar to the last one. Actually he fell in there so the car started shaking. He got up right away and instantly told me the address where we were headed – to a district in **Helsinki**, about 22 kilometers away. I couldn't understand the street well, because he stretched it infinitely. I asked again and he repeated the address, you could tell he was really trying to articulate the address. Just in case, I asked if the street was indeed in Helsinki, because the same street name could be in Helsinki, Espoo or Vantaa.

The gentleman acted fast and put on his seatbelt and after about a minute he slouched under it, as he fell asleep. He didn't even wake up when I was taking the highway exits at a good pace. I was afraid that he wouldn't wake up at all and that I would have problems with him when we finished and it was time to pay the bill.

Fortunately that wasn't the case. There were a few bigger holes near the destination, so I drove through them fast. The shaking helped and the man came back to reality from his dreams.

He paid the bill fast. After getting back his card he put it back in his wallet, then put his wallet in his chest pocket and quickly went out of the car, just saying: "*Moi-moi!*" And there he went. He came quickly and went quickly – like a beautiful woman with a man's money.

It seemed like a familiar condition. Sometimes you take a taxi to get home from the bar. When you arrive at your house, you try to pay the bill quickly, make sure all your belongings are in your pockets and that they would be there in the morning. You open the car door and already you're looking for the next door, so you could get inside. Usually you approach it at a 45-degree angle because gravity seems much stronger. After you get through the first door, you take the stairs at speed to reach the last door before finally getting to take a rest from the difficult night. It's like a final spurt after a marathon, where you have to use all your strength, focus 110% to get the result and reach the finish line tired but happy.

### The clown with a plastic bag and no sense of reality

**December**. I got a fare to an apartment building in **Olari, southern Espoo** at about 11 pm on a Friday. In relation to this story I got an idea. I wonder how many times the customers from this district have been problematic. If someone does some statistics on it, please tell me the result.

I drove to the building. Two old men exited the house. One of them had on glasses and an old jacket. About 60 years old, I think. Of course drunk, carrying a plastic bag. The other bloke was a bit more sober, I think he had been the host. The more adequate gentleman told me: "Hey, take home my pal."

Then the other clown sat in the back. I asked him: "Where do you live, where should I take you?" He said: "Umm, I know how to get there." I made a louder noise and insisted: "Where do you live?!" He told me the address. I hadn't realized that he wanted to go nearby, to **Matinkylä**.

I started to enter the address to the GPS when the drunkard already opened his mouth: "No-no! No need, I'll guide you!" "Yeah, yeah, you'll guide me," I responded to his proposal. I have seen those guides before, who forget where they are and where they're going.

We managed to drive for about 600 meters when the man suddenly had a need for nicotine. He moaned from the back seat: "Heeey, let's go to a nearby gas station and buy some cigarettes." "What cigarettes do you want," I asked. "Well buy me a big pack of red Pall Mall," he told me. "Well now you managed to pick a brand of smokes," I was thinking to myself. You would be better off breathing from a chimney.

So I went to the gas station and bought my pal a pack of Pall Malls. I gave him the receipt so he wouldn't complain. "No-no, I don't need it," he said. I told him: "Yes you do. I don't have to argue with you later when you discover that your drive cost a lot. Then you can see for yourself, where the money went."

We arrived at his house and started to deal with the bill. It was about 15 euros. Instead of looking for the money and paying the bill, the old man asked me: "Where am I? Where do I live?" I told him: "I don't know. You pointed that you live here," and insisted: "Come on, just pay the bill!" The old man gave me a tenner. I told him: "You need five more euros. You only gave me ten." Then he gave me two 2-euro coins. I told him again: "You need one more euro. The bill is 15.20." The moron told me: "Don't worry, I'll give it to you," and started looking for his money again.

After a few minutes of discovering the inside of his pockets, he found another 2-euro coin and gave it to me. I handed him a 1-euro coin back and he got ecstatic: "Oh, wow, I got some money back." I was thinking: "Yes you did, you waste of time. I even gave you a discount to leave the car quicker so I wouldn't have to see you again."

People who have lost touch with reality are tiring. They're wasted, they always argue, don't know where they are, who they are, where they're going or what they're doing. They waste time and just moan.

Like the delay hadn't been enough, he wanted to be escorted to his apartment. "Fuck you," I was thinking. I told him: "I'll escort you to the doorway, help you inside the house and that's it. You have to go on alone."

I got the clown in the building, along with his bag, so he would be in a warm room. I closed the outside door just in case, so he couldn't get back outside. I was pretty sure he hadn't been able to open the door from the inside, considering the condition he was in.

Because the yard was dark and there was a danger of hitting all kinds of bushes, curbstones, trash cans or the building itself, I tried to move carefully so I wouldn't damage the car.

The warning sensors on this car didn't work or it didn't have them. Once before in Helsinki I backed into a traffic sign. I was looking in the side mirrors and I hit it bang in the middle of the trunk lid. The car's electronic warning system didn't warn me of any dangers.

Anyway, I was trying to turn the car around in the yard, in front of the parking house, to get back to the street. As I was maneuvering, a loud thing, which looked like a Mazda made in the 80s, flew into the yard. The driver was from another era and impatient. He started to sound the horn right away! My shit was already boiling from the last idiot I had to deal with. Already another "V.I.P" had arrived and started annoying me.

I jumped out of the car and yelled at the moron: "Why the fuck are you beeping? Can't you see I'm trying to turn around and leave this damn yard?" The brainless man started arguing: "Yeah, yeah, back up, I want to get into the parking hall."

I stepped towards the ape, it seemed like a moment where I had had enough. I just wanted to let out all of the frustration that had collected dealing with these kinds of morons… But then my vision got clear, my blood started flowing and got from my arms to my brain. I calmed down and didn't let out my frustrations physically. I just told him: "You idiot, are you in such a hurry to get in that hall?! What's going to happen if you get there half a minute later – is your car going to fall apart?! Get some brains!" I sat in the car, turned it around and left the scene.

### The lumberjack who couldn't stop talking
**December**. Weekend. The evening got off to a great start. I was sitting in the **Leppävaara** taxi stand in **eastern Espoo**, near the **Helsinki-Espoo** border. A

drunk fellow approached my car in dirty, worn out clothes. The clown wanted to go to an apartment building in **Espoo center, Mid-Espoo** (about 12 kilometers). He had been drinking more than one day because when he got in, the stench of alcohol followed right away. It was about 7 pm, but he looked like an ice cream melting in the sun.

When I had turned out of the taxi stand, the old man started to doubt if he had enough money. I asked if he had it or not. "No, I SHOULD have it and if I don't have it on my card, I'll bring some money from my wife," he tried to calm me down. He told me not to worry.

Fortunately he acted calmly. As we were driving he explained how he works in the woods – how he chops down trees and which ones could he drag out himself, which ones not. I tried to look like I was listening and understood everything, just to keep the calm mood. I smiled and nodded to his stories, as I was listening to a drunk mumble.

At one point he got carried away with his forest-themed monologue. He was practically yelling at me from the passenger seat as he was spraying me with his fine saliva shower. I finally told her: "Sorry, I have to concentrate on the road. It's dark outside and it's raining. We could get into an accident." He tried to make a joke: "So we'll go to jail?" I told him: "No, we might get into an accident, not a jail." Then he told me that he had been held in the Espoo police station for four months. I asked him: "For what?" "Oh, a heavy narcotics crime," he commented shortly.

A few moments later he cleared his throat for a few times after his magnificent speech. Shit, it was like smelling a chimney – his breath smelled terrible.

Before arriving to the final destination I asked him about the exact place to stop: "Where is your house?" He pointed to an apartment building to the left of us and told me: "To that balcony, to that balcony." "What fucking balcony," I was thinking to myself. I confirmed my route: "Do I turn in this yard?" "Yes, right here! You can turn around right here then."

I accidentally drove a couple of meters past his doorway, because I couldn't understand which one was his. The woodchuck caught fire: "Damn it, not here, not so far! Brake, brake!" His reaction was like I had missed the right place by 200 meters.

I backed up a few meters and asked: "Is it better now?" "Yes-yes, this is good. This is great," he was satisfied.

The old man gave me his card and wanted me to enter his PIN. It was the correct PIN and the payment went through – fortunately he had enough money. Then I gave back his card. When he was receiving it, he made an attempt at humor again: "It's not my card. It's a criminal card."

He also wanted the receipt as he explained that he had to show it to his woman so she could see where the money went.

# FUNKY SENIORS

## The fashionable old woman

**October**. An afternoon on a regular workday. I was at the taxi stand in **Tapiola, southeast Espoo**. An old lady dressed like a biker mouse approached the car – she was wearing a purple jacket, a white soft cap with earflaps, like kids usually wear. She had on black track pants with white stripes on the sides. She was also wearing dark brown sunglasses with white frames. They covered half her face. A real fashion hit.

We drove to an apartment house in **Matinkylä, southern Espoo** (about 6.5 kilometers). The number of the doorway was 20.

When we arrived, I asked which house was hers. The fashionista explained that it was red and made out of bricks. Okay, I saw a red brick house on the left, a green apartment building on the right.

I turned left, but she suddenly started moaning: "Wrong direction, wrong direction!" "What do you mean, the red house is on the left," I asked. "No, the entrance is where the green house is." I didn't understand the logic. Why did she guide me to the red house when she was going to the green one? A brain of a mouse.

So I turned right. It was about 4-5 meters to her doorway. I accidentally drove past it, just a few meters. The fashionista started yelling again: "No-no-no, now you drove past it! The last doorway was mine!" "Okay, okay, got it, I'm sorry," I answered and backed up about 2 meters to the right doorway. She still felt it was necessary to instruct me: "Back up, back up and stop NOW! This is the right spot, this is the right spot!"

Some customers would drive to their bed if they could.

Anyway, after paying the bill, she praised me: "A very pleasant drive and a comfortable car." She added: "A very polite driver also. Thank you, thank you!" "You're welcome, glad you liked it," I answered.

## "Couldn't we drive to the elevator?"

**September**. A Friday afternoon. There was another old woman waiting for me at the taxi stand in **Espoonlahti, southwest Espoo**. She had a pushing cart for support. She wanted to go the elevator of the Soukka shopping center (about 2 kilometers) in a district nearby. You can take the elevator to get to the third floor to get to the shops or bars.

We arrived at the elevator. I stopped the car and waited for her to pay the bill. But nothing, she just sat there and stared at the elevator, which was about 2 meters in front of us.

So I asked her: "What now, is there a problem?" She asked me: "Why aren't we going?" Hearing that dumb question, I asked: "Where should we go, there's a wall in front of us." She still didn't understand what was going on: "But where's the elevator?" I explained her that it was right in front of the car, in the wall, on the left. "Oh, okay." Apparently she finally understood how to get to the elevator and started looking for money to pay the bill.

Sometimes when I drove with these kinds of people I asked myself: "Do they suffer regular concussions?"


### The woman who didn't know which hotel she was staying at and where her things were...

**December**. I got a fare from a private house in **southeast Espoo**. I picked up an old woman, at least 70 years old, and her daughter. They wanted to go to a hotel in **Ruoholahti, Helsinki**, but gave me the wrong address. I even asked them: "Are you sure there's a hotel there?" "Yes, yes, don't you know that hotel?!" they asked me, annoyingly. "No I don't. I only know one hotel by that name in that area and that is not located at that address," I told them.

On the way to the hotel I tried to figure out what building they were talking about. I wasn't aware of any other hotels by that name in the area.

When we got to Helsinki, I drove to the hotel that I thought was right. I asked them: "Is this your hotel?" "No-no, it doesn't seem like it," they told me. I asked: "Don't you know which hotel you are staying in?" "Well, we left during the day and now it's dark." The whole street in front of the hotel was well-lighted but they still didn't recognize it.

So I drove to the address they had given me.

We arrived at the destination, about a kilometer from the hotel. I asked: "So, where's the hotel?" They told me: "We don't know. *You* should know!" For fuck's sake, I have to know which fucking hotel you're coming from?!

I explained: "I'm not aware of any hotels here. There is only one hotel in Ruoholahti and we already went there. Let's drive back to where we came," I proposed.

We arrived at the hotel and I told them to ask at the reception if they were staying in that hotel.

The old woman returned and it turned out they were, in fact, staying in that same hotel.

Then they tried to apologize for giving me the wrong address and for having me drive to the wrong place.

The old woman, who had on all sorts of gold and glitter, paid the bill. I thought: "Well, they seem to be doing well, maybe they'll give a good tip for the unnecessary drive."

She paid the bill in cash, giving me 1.10 euros more than needed. I thought maybe they would leave that. The woman wasn't even thinking about leaving the car. She waited for me to give back the 1.10. I gave it back and we parted ways.

### The health guru in flip-flops

**October**. It was about 7 pm. I got a call to …kuja street in **Matinkylä, southern Espoo**. The number of the house had been entered as 999. Great. Basically the customer could come out of any house and I don't know where to wait. There wasn't a phone number in the order so I could be sure where I should be waiting.

I drove to the address. I waited in the general parking lot and started the meter. I had been waiting for 5 minutes but I couldn't see anyone. I was considering leaving and abandoning the fare. Right then I noticed a big lady, weighing about 100 kilograms, walking quickly next to an apartment building. I thought maybe that was my customer; why else would she be in such a hurry. I expected her to enter the car but instead she approached my window and told me: "There's a woman down there waiting for a taxi. Could you drive there? She can't get up herself." I told her: "Yes, okay, I'll be right there."

I reversed down the ramp. I saw an old woman, about 70 years old, sitting on a low wall, wearing flip-flops without socks. Well, why not let your feet breathe in the cozy October weather? The sitting woman was breathing heavily, even more than the one who had come up the ramp. I didn't know why.

I helped the old woman in the car and asked: "Where do you want to go?" " **Meilahti[73], Helsinki**," was her short answer.

When I saw her breathing heavily, I automatically thought she wanted to go to the Meilahti hospital. Just

---

[73] **Meilahti** – *A district in West-Helsinki. It is located about 4.5 kilometers to the northwest of the city center.*

in case I asked her: "To the hospital?" "No-no-no, not the hospital," she gave a panicking answer. "Where to then?" I asked again. "To …katu street," she told me. "Oh, okay," I let her know I knew where we were supposed to go.

When we arrived at the destination, she wanted to exit before we got to her house. She had gotten her breathing in order and told me: "I'll get out here. I'd like to take a walk." "Okay," I told her. I stopped the car and helped her out of the car after she paid the bill.

I was thinking: "Damn, you have to be really healthy to walk around in flip-flops in October."

## I want to see the "genius" who numbered the houses

**December**. An afternoon on a workday. **Soukka** district in **southwest Espoo**. I got a fare about 400 meters from the taxi stand, to an apartment building.

I drove there and had to find house number 5. When I arrived, I saw the layout of the houses in the parking lot. It was so confusing you could only throw snowballs at it. I couldn't understand shit, where was which house.

I'll describe it for you: When you enter the one-way street, then the first house on the left is number 16. If you go past it, there's house number 7. You have to find number 5. Logically it should be next to house number 7, right? It is next to number 7, but you could only get to the back of the house. But there aren't any doorways on the back. I wonder if the developer was drunk when numbering the houses.

Finally I saw how I could get in front of the number 5 building. Of course it was after I had ventured behind the house for some time. I raced to the doorways of the right house so the customers wouldn't have to wait any longer.

Like the numbering of the houses wasn't enough, somebody had thought that it would be a good idea to put a speed bump right in the MIDDLE of the parking lot. I didn't see it, because it was dark outside and I hit it doing about 40 km/h. Everything in the car went airborne, it was like being in a space station. The rear view mirror was knocked to the ceiling, like a crooked smile on a cartoon character. "For fuck's sake," I was cursing to myself. I would like to investigate the brain of some Finns, to see if there's anything there.

That wasn't all, though. I drove in front of the doorway, but the house was a few meters lower than the parking lot. To get to the doorway, you needed to drive down a narrow arc-shaped ramp.

I saw an old woman standing in front of the doorway. I jumped out of the car to help her get in. She asked: "Have you been here before? Your face is so familiar." I told her: "Maybe I have, but I can't remember every face. Hundreds of people come through the car in just a week."

I opened the door for her and wanted her to get in but instead she started yelling for his husband: "Come to the car now!" The genius had climbed half the ramp waiting for me. Walking wasn't one of his best skills any more, though. He slowly "slid" down the ramp like syrup. I couldn't drive closer to him either, I wouldn't have been able to open the car doors between the narrow walls. After all that I noticed that I hadn't started the meter. I flew into the car and started it.

After a few minutes the old man finally got to the car. Then he started saying that he had a taxi card. "Yeah, yeah, just get in the car, before the sun rises. "What," he couldn't understand. I repeated: "Just get in the car!" "Oh, okay. You know, I have my passport with me if you don't believe it's my taxi card!" "I don't care who's is it, as long there is money on it," I told him.

I packed the man on the front seat, the woman in the back and finally got going.

Guess where the destination was? Nearby, to **Espoonlahti** district, which was about 1.5 kilometers away. After all the adventure I went through – looking for the right house for 7-8 minutes, waiting for the old man to get in the car for 5-6 minutes, I got a fare that lasted for 5 minutes. Damn it, I was ecstatic of course.

So we drove to a mall in Espoonlahti. After the first 300 meters, the "newlyweds" managed to get into an argument. They started arguing if I should wait for them in the shopping center or not. The old man thought I should and the woman didn't. She thought they would take another cab. I told them that it made no difference to me. It was another 12-euro trip and lasted 15 minutes. I didn't say the last sentence of course, I didn't want to add oil to the fire.

The argued about it for half the trip until the man gave in. We managed to go 2 minutes in silence, until the old man started again: "Would you wait for us in front of the mall?" The old woman protested right away: "No, it isn't necessary. We'll take another taxi."

Well I finally managed to get them to the mall. They made clear that I wouldn't have to wait for them and I started packing the old man out of the car.

Finally I got rid of them and felt that my nerve system needed nicotine. What a fucking circus! If the evening started that way, what was going to happen before dawn?

## ADVENTURES WITH YOUNGSTERS

### "Take us behind the corner."

I was sitting at the taxi stand in **Matinkylä, southern Espoo** on a cold night in **February**. I was thinking about ending the shift and leaving. Suddenly a guy approached the car and asked: "Hey, can you take us behind that corner (while pointing with his finger) for a fiver?" I asked: "Why don't you walk if it's so close?" To the question, the young man answered quickly: "My friend is a bit drunk and he doesn't want to walk."

I thought for a moment and answered: "Okay, get in! I'll take you there. I was leaving anyway."

I took drove for about 300 meters, behind the corner of an apartment building for a fiver. I ended my shift after that. I was thinking to myself: "There are some weird people – they can't walk 300 meters, they would rather take a taxi. Well, if money isn't an issue, why not."

A similar story happened in Helsinki. A taxi driver had been sitting at the taxi stand with 7 taxis behind him. A tourist carrying a travel bag had arrived and asked the driver to take him to a certain hotel. The driver grabbed his bag, walked across the street and put it down in front of the doors of the hotel. The customer followed him, face full of surprise. The driver explained: "This is your hotel. Here you go!" The customer was surprised and embarrassed but he still gave the driver 10 euros for the "drive".

### The dude who was visiting a friend but didn't know the address

**May**. Afternoon. A young dude, a bit tipsy, approached my car at the taxi stand in **Kivenlahti, southwest Espoo**. When he got in the car, he announced: "You won't believe where we're going!" Slightly surprised, I asked: "Well, where then?" "**Tikkurila**[74]**, Vantaa.**" He was right, I didn't believe that I would get that lucky and get a long fare. Tikkurila is a small neighborhood in Vantaa. It is located about 40 kilometers to the east of Kivenlahti.

The fellow had been partying at a friend's place. But he forgot to ask his friend what the address was. He knew he lived in a high-rise building, but he didn't have any idea which floor and which apartment.

---

[74]*Tikkurila – a district of Vantaa, covers an area of about 1 square kilometer. It is located about 20 kilometers north of Helsinki.*

He had decided to leave the apartment to go to the store. On the way he found out that he had left his phone and all his other stuff at his friend's apartment. Now he couldn't call his friend to ask him to meet him somewhere and get him his stuff. So he came to the taxi stand and decided to go home, to Tikkurila.

He was hopeful that he would get back his stuff.

I took him to Tikkurila where he paid the bill without any problems – at least he had taken his card with him.


## Four happy but hungry "puppies"
Another night in **February**. Actually it was almost morning, about 3.30 am. I had just dropped some customers off in **Helsinki** from **Espoonlahti, south-west Espoo**. I decided to drive around in Helsinki, hoping I could get a new fare or see a customer.

I did get a fare. I was surprised because there were many other taxis driving around but I was the one to get it.

I drove to the address. When I arrived, I saw four happy "puppies" waiting for me on the street corner. They jumped in the air when they heard that I was their taxi – they needed to go **Espoo**, to a street with a funny name – **Tonttutytönkuja**. I started laughing when I heard the name. The guy sitting next to me commented my reaction: "Every time I say the address to the taxi driver, they always start laughing." "Of course they do, it's a funny name," I told him.

They were all about 18-20 years old. A bit tipsy, but funny and in a pleasant mood. The guy sitting behind me was quite drunk. The other two, a bit more adequate, talked very much, like women. Finally the bigger and fatter guy sitting between them asked the guy sitting on his right: "Hey, do you have some standard questions for the driver? For example, if you get in a taxi, you ask the driver how the night was going or if there had been many customers, how long he had been driving and so on?"

I started laughing at the question, because half of the customers ask EXACTLY those questions. It was true this time too. We made a deal that all the guys could ask me one "standard question".

We got to Espoo and drove towards the Niittykumppu district – the three guys sitting in the back decided they need to go to a McDonald's and get some food.

We went to the drive-in. The guys ordered their food after yelling some stupid shit to the cashier. I was forced to close the windows so it wouldn't get impolite.

After ordering we turned around the corner to get the food from the window. We saw five cars waiting before us. Seeing that, the guys decided that they had spent enough money that night and that they would head home. So we left without buying the food and I took them home with empty hands and stomachs.

### Three girls, a carton of beer and an industrial district

I remember a party of girls from this nightly shift in **February**. I picked them up at about 3 am, in **Matinkylä, southern Espoo**, in front of the **Iso Omena**[75] shopping center.

I saw three girls, about 20 years old, approaching me from a bar. They had a carton of beer with them. They were all decently tipsy. When they got close, I exited the car and seeing the carton, I asked politely: "Maybe you want to put the box in the trunk?" One of them snapped back at me: "No, we won't put anything in the back!" Well, okay. "It seems like you haven't gotten any for some time, why else would you be so frustrated," I snapped. The voice and reaction of the girl predicted a challenging and interesting trip.

---

[75] „Big Apple" in Finnish

*10. Iso Omena shopping center in Matinkylä.*

Two girls got in the back and the third sat next to me. I politely closed the doors after they got in and entered myself. I asked where they were going. They all answered together: "**Myyrmäki**[76], **Vantaa**." It was about 22 kilometers east from us. I asked to specify: "Where exactly, which street?" They responded arrogantly again: "I don't know, just drive to Myyrmäki!" I calmly asked again: "Where exactly? Myyrmäki is big." Actually it isn't.

---

[76]***Myyrmäki*** – *A district of Vantaa, covers an area of about 2.7 square kilometers. It is located about 14 kilometers northwest of Helsinki.*

To my question, one of the ladies called a friend of hers and asked the exact street name. But it didn't help us. She couldn't get enough information on the exact place we had to go to.

I looked up Vantaa on the GPS and entered Myyrmäentie. It looked like it existed but I didn't exactly know where. My brains were pretty soft from the nightly adventures and I couldn't put together the right route in my head.

During the drive, it turned out that we had to go to Myyrmäki train station. I told the girls: "You can show me how to get there." In between all the chatter, some unsatisfied complaining came from the back: "How is it possible that a taxi driver doesn't know how to get to Myyrmäki train station?" I told them: "Sorry, I'm a taxi driver in Espoo. I don't have to know that." Actually I should have known. But I had to excuse myself somehow and make life a little easier for myself. My tired brain didn't think about asking the address from an information line. It was actually "Ratatie 1".

After driving for about half an hour, we arrived at the train station. I was hoping to get rid of the arrogant girls. It turned out that someone was joining our party. He could show me where to take the girls. But he had another girl with him. It was one passenger too many.

The guy asked me if I would take one extra passenger but I refused. I didn't need the risk. Hearing my negative answer, the companion of the guy started moaning that she didn't want to go with the girls sitting in the car.

After about 3-4 minutes of arguing I told them: "Just decide –, are you staying here or are you going somewhere. I don't have time to wait for you while you debate what to do."

They quickly decided that the group in the car would continue with me. They promised to find out what was the exact address of the destination. One of the girls called her friend again. The friend told her the address but the girl couldn't understand it. The person on the other end of the call probably told the girl to give the phone to me. The young lady gave me her phone and told me to listen to the street name.

I heard a drunk male voice but I couldn't understand what he said either. I gave the phone back and recommended sending the address via SMS. That way I could see the correct spelling of the address.

The guy did send the address. I searched for it in the GPS but didn't find it right away because I had accidentally left a letter out. I told the girls that I still couldn't find the right address. One of the pussies moaned back at me from the back seat: "Just give me the damn GPS! I'll enter the address myself!!" I told her to go fuck herself in my thoughts.

I entered the address a second time and found the right place. I saw that it was a long way to go – about 17 kilometers. To be sure, I asked them if they are certain it was the right place, because it's far away. They told me: "Yes, we're sure! It might be far away." They added that the place was located in **Tikkurila**, a small district in Vantaa.

I turned onto the **Kehä III** highway from Myyrmäki. My GPS was so slow calculating the route that I passed the right exit. I needed to stay in the right lane when I got to the highway and take the first exit. When the GPS had completed its calculations, it told me to take the next exit, which was about 4 kilometers away.

I stopped the meter and the situation on the back seat got restless again. The girl sitting next to me was the most peaceful and polite. I forgot to mention that when we're in the train station, she offered to buy me food to compensate her friends' moaning. The caring girl took out her phone and turned on her GPS. We compared the routes on our GPSs and it seemed like we were going the right way.

When I had taken the wrong exit and right away turned back to the highway, the girls' male friend called again. He asked where we were. One of the girls in the back complained: "Bla-bla-bla, fuck, we're lost again! The taxi driver doesn't know where we are and where we're going." After the complaint, she gave me the phone.

A guy asked me where we were and started guiding me to the destination. When he was explaining, he got stuck himself. He gave the phone to another guy. As I understood, he was a taxi driver also. The colleague explained: "You drive past one exit and the other, then you turn up and left and right and there's an office of a company, etc…" After I listened to the direction I told him: "You can guide me but I can't memorize it all, if I have to take so many turns. I have entered the address in the GPS and hopefully we can find the right place." I explained: "I just drove past the right exit and now we're just taking some extra time to get there." He understood that everything was under control and the call ended.

After about 5-6 minutes, we arrived at an office of a company. Next to it was another company, without a building, just a big tarmac lot with some building cabins on it.

We drove to the gate of the lot where the guy from the train station was waiting for us.

The girls from the back seat got out right away. The calmest and politest girl next to me paid the bill. She apologized for her friends' behavior. After that, she thanked me for the ride and asked: "Will we see you again?" I told her: "If you're from **Espoonlahti**, we're bound to meet again."

After the last girl got out, I drove to a nearby street to have a smoke. While inhaling the calming feeling from the cigarette I thought about the situation – to drive to some lot in the middle of nowhere at 3 am for 75 euros with a carton of beer... Must be a great experience. Well, everybody has their own fun – some go to the amusement park, some go to an industrial park to drink beer.

## The crazy Pippi Longstocking jumping in front of the casino

I had just taken a customer to **Vantaa** and I decided to drive to **Espoo** through the city center of **Helsinki**. You can sometimes find a customer driving through there.

I drove slowly past a casino (there is only ONE casino in Helsinki, it is located in the city center), I saw a crazed redhead waving her arms on the side of the street. She kept running from one place to another. I saw that and thought that maybe she was trying to hail a taxi. Although there was a taxi stand right across the street, where there were other people waiting for a car.

I stopped the car in the middle of the street to ask her if she wanted a taxi. The girl jumped in the car without replying anything. She started talking right away: "Damn, that taxi driver was a moron for not picking me up!" I explained her: "Actually I shouldn't have picked you up on the street also, if the taxi stop is right across the street. It's not fair and you can just take three steps if you want to get a taxi." The information didn't get through to the mad adrenaline junkie. The girl kept "boiling." She must have had a bad night. She kept illustrating that all taxi drivers were jerks and men were jerks and life was shit anyway. I tried telling her: "Everything is okay! You're in a taxi now and soon you'll be home. Everything is in order!" My talk didn't work. She kept mumbling in the backseat.

After we had finally arrived at her house and she had paid her bill, she turned her frown upside down. She finally "opened up" and said she was happy and grateful for picking her up and getting her home, also the service had been good.

### The student who got the districts confused
**July**. I picked up a 20-year-old guy from a nightclub in **Tapiola, southeast Espoo** on an early morning on a Sunday. He wanted to go to his dorm in **Otaniemi**, the district next to us. As it was an early weekend morning, he was quite drunk.

He told me a story. He had walked from **Helsinki** to Tapiola (about 10 kilometers) during the night, but he wanted to go to Otaniemi. He had just gotten lost.

So he had begun to walk back from the exit to Tapiola.

On the way to town he started doubting if it was the right way to Otaniemi. So he turned back and walked to Tapiola.

He ordered a taxi to the local nightclub to make sure he got to his dorm. I asked him how he could get lost in such a simple place.

The young man explained that he had been painting a house the day before. After he finished he thought that he would have a couple of beers. As usual a few beers turned into a few more beers. He explained: "Every time I go out to have a few beers, the evening gets interesting and I get into adventures. And when I try to get drunk and party hard, it doesn't usually work out."

This time the two beers had been enough to last until early morning.

*11. The "male road" from Otaniemi to Tapiola (miesten = "men's")*

*"You know why you're more drunk than I am?" "Well?" "You didn't take a break."*

**December.** I picked up two drunk guys, about 23-24 years old, from an office building in some business grounds in **Keilaranta, southeast Espoo**. They wanted to go to **Lauttasaari**, on the border of **Espoo** and **Helsinki** (about 5 kilometers). One of the guys was more drunk than the other. The wasted guy sat next to me and the half-sober one got in the back.

The following conversation took place in the car, as the more sober guy said: "You know, this is the first time I'm sober than you." The guy next to me answered: "Well yeah, I don't know how it happened or how you managed it." The other guy responded from the back: "Well you didn't take a break." The guy in the front agreed: "Well I guess that's true." The first guy added: "And another thing, your head can't take it." The friend agreed: "Yup, I have to train more, I have to train more."

When we got to Lauttasaari, we arrived at an interesting spot. There was a narrow overpass ahead of us, not much wider than my car. There were some roadwork going on and we got a red light. The sober man then said: "Fuck, it's like living in a metropolis, when I try to drive home at night!" He went on and on: "Shit, every night the fucking builders come and start working, PRRRRR-PRRRRR! I don't get it, what are they doing during the daytime? Why do they have to do it at night," he said, properly irritated.

Finally, after we got a green light, we got to the apartment building where they wanted to go. They paid the bill without any problems and vanished into the darkness in a good mood and wishing me a good night.


### "Umm, isn't this a large taxi-bus?!"

**September.** I was sitting at the taxi stand in **Tapiola, southeast Espoo** on a weekend. It was about 5 am. Some people approached the car: two girls and four wasted guys. Their average age must have been about 20.

The party was probably coming from a nearby nightclub, where they had probably consumed several interesting substances. I think the substances had gone to their head. They all wanted to get in the car, although I had only five seats. I would have been the seventh person in the car.

The two guys wanted to get in the front seat, it seemed logical to them. First, one of the guys sat down and then the other sat in his lap with his feet out of the door.

It was clear they were all completely wasted because none of their talk made sense.

Seeing what they were trying, I asked: "Wait, wait. What are you doing? You all want to get on my car?" Then the small-brained girls asked: "Umm, aren't you the big taxi-bus?!" I asked, ironically: "Do you see a bus?" and added: "It's a regular car, not a bus!"

The guys next to me didn't understand the information given to them. They were sitting there like a couple in love. I had to use coercion to get them out. After talking about it for a moment they decided that some would get on the taxi and some would walk. According to the rules, four people stayed in the car. We drove to an apartment building about 800 meters away.

After that fare, I was seriously wondering: "I don't get it. You have less than a kilometer to go on a pleasant autumn morning. You could get your head clear in the fresh air, but no – you have to take a taxi and act foolish in it. What are they teaching you in schools that you're such morons?"

## "Why the fuck are you damaging the car?!"

An early morning on a weekend in **October**. I got a fare to the local hotel in **Tapiola, southeast Espoo**.

I drove to the parking lot, about 30-40 meters from the main door. There were two guys standing in the lot, about 22-24 years old. I stopped next to them to ask if they had ordered a taxi. They told me they had and one of the guys sat in the car right away, without saying anything.

The conversation started with the dude in the back. I asked: "What's the number of the order?" I needed to know if they were my customers. He told me 38. I calmly told him: "I'm sorry, that's not the right number. I have another number." Then he guessed again – 48. I calmly told him again, even laughing a bit: "Sorry, that's not correct either." I asked him to get out of the car. The correct number was 85.

I offered the guys: "I'll go to the door of the hotel. I'll ask the reception if anybody is coming and if not, I'll pick you up." The guy sitting in the car started boiling and yelling: "What the fuck?! I ordered a fucking taxi!" He got out and slammed the door after him. Since I had been dealing with all kinds of clowns for the previous 14 hours, I reacted – I jumped out of the car and yelled at him: "Why the fuck are you damaging the car?! Fuck, is it the car's fault that you didn't get the taxi?!" I continued: "Why do you need to bang the door?! Do you close your doors at home like that?!" The fool looked at me with a stupid face and couldn't say anything.

I got in the car and drove to the main door of the hotel. I asked the reception if anybody had ordered a taxi. They told me that nobody had.

I cancelled the order and left the parking lot, leaving the two imbeciles waiting for their taxi. A typical night on a weekend.


### "I'm going to get laid today!!"

**July.** **Olari** district in **southern Espoo**. A 20 year-old energetic, chatty guy came into the car from an apartment building. When he sat down, he introduced himself, shook my hand and told me the address: "**Mankkaa!**[77]" It was the district next to us. He added: "Let's go get my girl." Then he started humming a melody, quietly repeating: "I'm going to get laid today, I'm going to get laid..."

---

[77] **Mankkaa** – *a neighborhood of private houses in Espoo, located about 17 kilometers to the north-west of Helsinki*

We got to some woods in Mankkaa, where a gravel road took us to a lone summer house. A big party was going on. Some people were outside, in front of the house, with a couple of beautiful ladies among them.

I parked the car and we started waiting for the girl. I asked him: "Which one of them is yours?" He told me: "I don't know. I'm not sure…" "What do you mean, you don't know?" I said. "Well I have seen her only once and don't really remember," he told me. "Oh, okay," I replied.

After a minute one of the beauties arrived. He got in the backseat to flirt with the girl.

Then I took the young couple back to Olari to enjoy their quality time.

## The best "athletes" come from sports bars

**October**. I got a fare to a local sports bar at about 11 pm in **Matinkylä, southern Espoo**. It was located 400 meters from the temporary taxi stand. It was temporarily there because a nearby bridge was being widened. It was originally right in front of the bar.

Two guys, about 25 years old, came out of the bar and got into the car. The taller of the two, wearing some track pants and cap, sat next to me and the "athlete" who was wearing a jacket and some jeans got in the back. I asked where we were going and I got the address – it was in **Olari** (about 2.5 kilometers).

Everything was okay at the beginning. We had driven about 400-500 meters when the guy behind me calmly asked: "Where has the taxi stand been moved in Matinkylä from the sports bar?" I explained: "It was moved to the Fortuna pub because of the Piispansilta roadwork (the sports bar was next to the bridge)." The guy sitting next to me asked: "Where are you from?" I told him: "From Estonia." "From Tallinn?" one of the "athletes" asked. I told him that I was from the western part of Estonia. "Oh, okay," the athlete responded and continued with a new tone: "You're saying the taxi stand needs to be moved from the sports bar to the Fortuna?!" I calmly explained: "No, it's not my decision. I'm just saying that the stand was moved because of some construction work. It's at the same place it used to be." The athlete kept looking for problems: "YOU are going to tell me, WHERE the taxi stand is?! Who the fuck are you?!" He was boiling. I asked him: "What is your problem? I'm just saying where the taxi stand has been moved. I haven't moved it." He poured gasoline on the fire: "You? You shut the fuck up!" raising his voice and looking at me with anger.

I couldn't understand what the hell was going on and asked the moron: "What the hell? What is your problem?!" "Do you even know who I am?!" he asked me. I told him: "No I don't and I don't care." Then I asked again: "Hey, what is your problem?" I was thinking about stopping the car and throwing them out. Or else it might get out of hand.

I decided to continue driving, because the destination was only a kilometer away. Just in case, I put my hand on the pepper spray in my pocket, just in case the situation escalated. The guy in the back tried to calm the brainless ape: "Hey, calm the fuck down."

We arrived at the destination without fighting. Right when I stopped the car, the athlete next to me exited and walked away fast. The calm guy in the back paid the bill and apologized for his friend. He asked me to add an extra 3 euros to the bill, for compensation. I did. Not that the 3 euros made me forget. I should have sprayed the pepper spray in the moron's face and hit him a couple of times. Then I would have been able to forget the situation. But a taxi driver can't do anything to these spoiled shit heads.

## "I fell asleep on the train..."

**November.** Early morning. It was about 6 am.

A young fellow approached my car in **Espoo center, Mid-Espoo**. He had a big problem. He explained: "I only have 20 euros, would take me towards **Leppävaara** for as long as possible?" I told him: "Sure, I'm not going to leave you here in the cold. And where would I drop you off before Leppävaara? I can't leave you on the highway. Get in!" The actual price to Leppävaara would have been about 25 euros.

*12. A district in Leppävaara called Veini (wine).*

He explained that he came from Helsinki and he was a bit tipsy. He had fallen asleep on the train and drove past the Leppävaara station. Fortunately somebody had woken him up before the Espoo center stop. One of the passengers wanted to exit in Espoo center and pushed the stop button. The sound woke him up. He had opened his eyes and looked out the window. He couldn't understand: "What kind of ghetto am I in now?" Then he had realized that he was in Espoo center and quickly left the train.

You can sometimes see these lost customers in the morning.

### The freezing girl without money

**November**. Nighttime during a regular workday. The best description for this shift is: "The show must go on!"

After I had taken a pregnant lady in a hurry to the hospital in **Jorvi**[78], I decided to go to the nearest stand to wait for the ETL. I didn't get it, because I got a fare to the local mall.

It was nighttime and dark. The parking lot of the mall wasn't well lightened. It was practically dark. The

---

[78] *Jorvi – a little district between Espoo center and Viherlaakso.*

only light source was the streetlights on one side of the parking lot.

I made a big circle in the parking lot when I saw a dim silhouette waving at me. I approached it and it turned out to be a pretty lady. She got in and started complaining that she was so cold because she had been waiting for the bus for the last two hours. It didn't come and when she ordered a taxi time before, it had left... I remembered that there was a notification on Data at about 2am – there was a customer without money near the mall. I asked the girl if she was the one. "Yes, it's me," she admitted and added: "I ordered a taxi but the driver wouldn't pick me up because my card wouldn't work and I couldn't pay the bill." I don't know if she had taken a taxi there and the driver notified the dispatcher or how the driver knew that her card didn't work. She told her version – she had called a taxi but told the driver her card didn't work and the driver had just left her there. Anyway the girl, about 20 years old, added that her mother would pay the bill when we arrive at her house in **Soukka**, southwest Espoo (about 15 kilometers).

On the way to the Kehä II circuit the girl asked me to stop so she could have a smoke. I offered her a light. She finished it in three drags and calmed down a bit. I could see that she was in shock, because she had been left freezing in a bus stop in the middle of nowhere.

We drove to Soukka, where the mother met us and paid the bill, like she said. The girl was happy to get to her warm home. Everything was good.

When I had dropped her off, the Data was displaying another notification – the cards weren't working AGAIN because of maintenance. It was probably the reason why the girl couldn't pay (she probably tried to get some cash from an ATM before) and why the taxi had left her there.

## The three clowns with great imagination

**November**. An evening on a regular workday. I got a fare from **Haukilahti, southern Espoo**.

When I got to the address, I saw three guys, about 18-20 years old, smoking in front of the house. I think they weren't just smoking cigarettes, they were "smoking" some stuff. They seemed very fun and humorous guys.

When they entered the car I asked where they were headed. "Teleportti," one of them told me. "Where?!" I asked, as I started laughing. "To where

**Storyville**[79] is." "Oh, okay, now I know," I answered. I thought what he meant by Teleportti. It seemed like he was under some influence and imagined that he would teleport to the jazz club.

When I had turned on the highway from Haukilahti, driving towards **Helsinki**, one of the clowns asked: "Are we on **Tuusulanväylä**[80] right now?" I told him: "Yeah, we're just passing the airport[81]!" Everybody started laughing at the dumb question and answer. The same clown asked me: "Can you fit on the road?" There were four lanes going both ways. I told him: "Well I think I can. It's complicated but I can handle it." "Oh, that's good," he said, satisfied for a moment. Then he kept asking: "What's your name?" I told them: "I don't remember." Everybody started laughing again. They started guessing my name. They guessed my name was Antti. I told them: "No, I'm not Antti." They kept guessing. To every guess, I said: "No, no, no, not that and not that." Finally I told them the "truth": "My name is **Kramer**[82]." "What Rain-

---

[79] *Storyville – a jazz club in the city center of Helsinki.*
[80] *Tuusulanväylä - it's the highway in the east connecting Helsinki and Tuusula through Vantaa.*
[81] ***The Helsinki-Vantaa International** airport is located in Vantaa, near the Tuusulanväylä.*
[82] ***Kramer** – a character from the famous comedy show Seinfeld.*

er? Or Reiner? Oh, Reinar?" they kept guessing. "No, Kreimer, it's spelled Kramer," I introduced the old comedy to the younger generation. "Don't you know him," I asked the clowns. "No, we haven't seen the show," the guys told me. "Of course you haven't. You were made when it was popular," I answered, laughing ironically.

When we arrived at Storyville, the party got out of the car. The clown sitting in the front, who seemed like the most high, dropped a Koff beer can when he was leaving. I yelled: "Hey, you left your lemonade!" He turned around and took the red can. He thanked me and wished me a good night. I responded with the same. It was a fun ride. You don't screw with friends and pleasant customers.

### From the national theatre into the "woods" with two suspicious guys

**November**. Morning on a weekend. It was about 4 am. I had dropped of some customers in **Helsinki** and got a new fare – to the ***Kansallisteatteri***[83]. The theatre is located right in the city center near the train station.

---

[83]*Kansallisteatteri* – *the national theatre of Finland, the oldest one in Finland, established in 1872.*

I thought I would pick up a lady in a ball dress and a gentleman in a suit who had just watched an opera and wanted to go home. I didn't realize it was 4 am.

I called the number given in the order. A young bloke answered the call. I told him that I would be there in 6-7 minutes. He was fine with it. I rethought who the potential customers were. I thought they must be a young couple wanting to get home.

I arrived at the theatre. Two guys, about 20-22 years old approached the car in the dark alley. Baggy pants, winter coats and ski hats on.

*13. A view of the National Theatre of Finland in Helsinki.*

I asked them: "Did you order a taxi?" "Yeah, we're the one you spoke to on the phone," one of the guys told me. "Okay, get in," I told them and added: "Where are we going?" I presumed that it would be a short stint in the city. One of the guys told me: "**Järvenpää** (about 40 kilometers to the north of Helsinki)." I was surprised and asked: "What, Järvenpää?!" "Yeah, Järvenpää. You get to drive a little," one of them said.

I was thinking suspicious thoughts. I had picked up two young guys dressed like that from a dark alleyway, who wanted to go 40 kilometers to the north at 4 am… I thought for a bit and said: "Okay, let's go." I hadn't been there in a while, I thought.

One of the guys sat next to me, the other got in the back. The guy in the back fell asleep in a couple of minutes, as he fell sideways on the back seat. I thought: "Well, one man down, one to go."

I didn't even notice that the guy in the back fell asleep. His friend noticed him and told me: "Look, I think my friend fell asleep." I looked over my shoulder and confirmed his fact.

About 3-4 minutes later we passed an ambulance that had its sirens on. He woke up, looked around for a bit to see where we were and then fell asleep again. I thought: "Sleep, sonny, there's a long way to go."

When we reached the highway, the guy sitting next to me, also fell asleep. I thought that it would be a pretty decent bill, about 70 euros. I was thinking if they had the money or would they just run away. I was planning my moves. I put together a plan, that if they would run, what would I do – what would I take from the car and how could I catch one of them.

Fortunately the drive ended calmly.

When we arrived at their house, the guy next to me paid the bill. Then he woke up the guy in the back and told him to go home. He was so dizzy that he almost fell when he got out of the car. Luckily he stumbled with skill, he grabbed the car door with his arms. I worried that he would break his ribs. But no, nothing happened. After half a minute of wiggling, he got up and stumbled in to the darkness, toward the door of a private house. The other guy left too and I drove into the weekend's crisp air.


### The same morning. Järvenpää vol 2. The bald guy and the annoying guy

I had just dropped off the two guys coming from the **National Theatre** in **Helsinki**. I was planning to go back to Helsinki but I got a fare after a few kilometers.

The order said that I needed to drive into the town to a hairdresser. Interesting. I entered the address to the GPS to see how far was the customer, would it be worth the drive. I have had situations where you drive to get a customer who is 15 minutes away, and when you arrive there aren't any customers there and you made an unnecessary drive.

The GPS said I had eight minutes to go before I got to the customer. I was satisfied. I would call the customer when driving to see if he still wanted the taxi and where exactly was located.

A male voice answered. I was given information that he was waiting in front of the hairdresser's and that he was wearing black pants. I gave him information about the car so he wouldn't take another taxi. That happens pretty often too.

There were actually two guys waiting for me in front of the salon. One of them was 2 meters tall, 1.5 meters wide, a bald bonehead. There was a skinny nerdy guy with glasses next to him, about 165 centimeters tall and wearing jeans, about 35 years old. It was a pretty funny picture. I wasn't really comfortable with picking up a two-meter Goliath at 5.30 am in the middle of nowhere. I thought: "What the hell – life is an adventure – let's do it and see what happens!"

The guys got in the car – the baldy got in the back and the nerd sat next to me. The baldy announced with a dry voice: "My friend is going to **Järvenpää** and is paying separately. Then we'll continue." "Got it," I said, and we started going.

It turned out that the baldy had just been freed by the police – he had been interrogated for the last four hours. The nerd asked him: "What did you do?" The baldy, who turned out to be just over 20 years old, said: "Oh, just a heavy accounting law violation." The nerd started telling him what to do: "Don't do stupid stuff. Be a normal person and live in accordance with the law like most people." The baldy agreed: "I guess I should, before I go to jail."

We arrived at the nerd's house. He found his card from his ragged jeans and paid the bill. He thanked me for getting him home and stumbled to his house.

The baldy exhaled in relief: "Thank the gods that we got rid of him. He was already annoying me in front of the salon. Thank you for picking me up. All the other taxis I tried to stop slowed down but when they saw me, they accelerated and drove off." I laughed and thought to myself: "No wonder they drove off, when a bonehead looking like a killer tries to stop them." I continued the drive towards the small town of **Kerava**, about 12 kilometers away.

Baldy was actually friendly. He told me his adventures of the day: "I woke up in the police station. Then they started interrogating me. If that ended, I asked the cops to take me to the train station so I could get home." They didn't bother and had just given him directions how to get to the station. Baldy had started walking but got lost. Finally he called a taxi. Again, a taxi is the hero of the day.

I took him near Kerava, to a random, dark field. A coffee shop was there, which was closed. His car and stuff was parked there too. People who value their health and life wouldn't walk there after the sun sets. I think people even drive past the place as fast as they can.

Baldy paid the bill, gave a tip of 1.60 euros for the good trip and for charging his phone and we parted our ways. I went towards the highway to get to Helsinki. The clock showed 4:38 on a Saturday morning.

After that fare really wanted to cool myself down with a cold beer.For example an ice cold Koff beer from the nearby Sinebrychoff factory in Kerava. Unfortunately all I could have was an unhealthy cigarette and some warm bottled water.

## The "reasonable" guys from Kivenlahti

**December.** Morning on a weekend. I picked up two guys, about 23-25 years old, from **Kivenlahti, southwest Espoo**. They wanted to go to a neighborhood called **Latokaski**, which was about 4 kilometers away.

After 2-3 kilometers, on an intersection they got into an argument. They started arguing who would go where. One of the clowns wanted to go back to Kivenlahti, the other wanted to go to Latokaski. We stood there for 3-4 minutes until the nightly bus came, which forced us to move. The movement forced the guys to decide quickly. The decided that we would go to Latokaski, so we did.

We arrived at the right address. It turned out that one of the clowns still didn't want to leave the car. He wanted to go to **Espoonlahti**, next to Kivenlahti, to some girl – at 4.30 am... The other guy had had enough. He told me to take him to the district of **Eestinmalmi**, about 3 kilometers away, where he lived. So a whole other place.

We drove to Eestinmalmi with both of them. The guy who wanted to go home was a lot more adequate than the one who wanted to go Espoonlahti. The

Eestinmalmi gentleman told me before leaving the car: "I'd bet that my friend won't remember a thing tomorrow. He probably won't remember which way we drove and how he got to Espoonlahti." I laughed and recommended: "Show your friend the taxi receipt. He'll remember what he did. Let him calculate how a three-kilometer trip cost as much as a 10-kilometer one."

## "If I don't have enough money, I'll pay you in liquor"

**May**. Weekend. I picked up a guy from an intersection in **Olari, southern Espoo** at about 2am. He wanted to go to the **Mankkaa** district nearby, about 4-5 kilometers. Before getting in the car he told me that he only had 15 euros. He asked if I could take him as far towards Mankkaa, as he could get for the money. I told him that I would take him. I couldn't leave him a few kilometers from his house in the middle of the night. He was so satisfied with the answer that he promised to pay me extra when we arrived. He told me that he didn't have any money but certainly had beer and he could give me that. I was fine with it.

I asked him why he didn't have any money, considering he was coming from a bar. He explained that he had recently separated from his wife. To be more exact, her wife had left him and taken half their assets with her. He had bought her a car, expensive jewelry and clothes before the divorce. The woman had taken off with all her stuff plus half the assets worth a million euros, to be with another man. She had cost him quite a bit. So he didn't have any money to even take a taxi to get home.

We arrived at his house. He insisted that I would enter with him to his apartment because he had promised me beer. I thought, why not. I just wanted to see how and where this guy lived.

After looking around in his messy apartment he didn't find any beer or money, but he found a coffee liqueur. He gave it to me in gratitude. Still helpful.


## "I'm going to see my friends, you take the kids home!"

**December.** Evening on a regular workday. I picked up a guy, 17-18 years old and three little angels, about 7-10 years old, from the stand near the **Barona Arena**[84]. It was an entertainment center in **Tapiola**,

---

[84]*Barona Arena - is an arena in Espoo, located by the ice rink and the fair center, in Tapiola.*

**Espoo**. They wanted to go to the **Tapanila** district in **Helsinki**, about 21 kilometers away.

When we got near **Leppävaara**, the guy told me to take him to the train station. He explained that he was going to meet some friends and I had to take the kids home. A typical Finnish attitude.

The guy gave me the kids' address and I took them where they had to go. Fortunately everything had been well organized. When I arrived, the father of the children came out, paid the bill and I could turn back towards Espoo without any problems.


## Even a gang member is afraid of his Finnish wife

**July**. Olari district in **southern Espoo** again. I picked up an ex-gang member at night. He wanted to go to **Helsinki**.

He was bald, full of tattoos, had a flat head and an athletic build, but was friendly and polite.

On the way to the destination he worried about whether he would get in his house. He supposedly had an angry wife, who maybe wouldn't let him in. I asked: "What do you mean, YOU are afraid of your wife, you look like a fighter." "Yes I am," he admitted. Then he added: "I can be the man on the street. I can stab, shoot, fight but when I go home, I'm just a nice boy who agrees with everything."

He explained that Finnish women were all furious at home because they think that they decide everything. Then, after a little pause, he admitted: "Actually they do. They are the boss. You can't beat up your wife, because when you do, everybody turns against you." He added: "That's why Finnish women are so hot-blooded. Every Finnish woman wants to get a decent guy, not some sheep," and put a question in the air: "But where is the border between a sheep and a bull?"

## The mistress, the tired builder and the tired youngsters

**September**. A night during a workday. I got a customer from the stand in **Kivenlahti, southwest Espoo**. It was a tired Finnish builder. Yeah, it seems there are some builders that are Finnish, not every builder is from **Estonia**. Okay, okay, just a little joke.

He was about 25-30 years old. He told me that he had gone in a bar with some friends but got too tired. Just tired from work and he couldn't spend the next 10 hours in a bar. I could see that he really was tired because during the 10-minute drive he constantly fought to not fall asleep.

I dropped him off and got another fare. I drove to the **Suomenoja** district, west of **Olari**. I picked up a blonde lady from a private house, about 40-45 years old. He was accompanied by a gentleman in a robe, about the same age. They didn't seem like a married couple.

The lady wanted to go to **Viheri**[85]**, eastern Espoo** (about 15 kilometers). It seemed like she had had a tiring day also, because she also fought not to fall asleep. When we got to Viheri, she was still trying not to fall asleep. She was helped by the speed bumps, which are placed everywhere in that neighborhood.

When I had dropped off the lady, I turned back the way I came – towards Viheri center. When I turned onto the street, a guy in a long sleeved shirt waved at me. He was with his girl. I stopped and the guy, about 20 years old, said: "Listen, could you take us to the Alepa store, about a kilometer from here. Damn it's cold outside. The thing is, I don't have any money, just some coins. Would you take us?" I asked him how much he had. He went through his pockets

---

[85]***Viheri*** *– a district Viherlaakso*

and came up with a handful of coins - about three or four euros. I thought that I couldn't leave them out in the cold. And I'm going there anyway, I don't want to drive for free. I decided to not start the meter but I would take the three or four euros. I told him: "Get in. I can't leave you here in the middle of the night." And it really was cold, maybe just 5 degrees Celsius.

So we drove for a kilometer or so. He thanked me the whole way: "I really appreciate it. Thank you for picking us up. It's so cold outside." I told him: "Don't worry about it. Now you're in a warm car and everything is fine," and tried to approach the situation with some humor: "you have your girl with you to keep you warm. How could you be cold?" He had lost all hope and told me: "No, even the girl's warm body and soft hands won't keep me warm – it's just so cold."

I dropped them off at his house where he still thanked me several times. He shook my hand and wished me a good night. I had a good feeling, because I had helped someone out. It doesn't matter that I didn't make much money for it.

# A COUPLE OF STORIES USHERING IN PART TWO OF THE BOOK

## *"Haista paskaa, sä saatana homo!"*[86]

A Finnish-Swedish colleague, Doggy, had gotten a fare near **Matinkylä**, **southern Espoo** to a private house.

He got there but because it was dark outside, he didn't see the numbers on the houses. So he kept driving back and forth on the street to find the client and the right house.

Finally an old hag dragged herself out of a yard, waved to Doggy and yelled: "Damn it, come here!"

When she got on the car, straight away she started an "enthusiastic" conversation with Doggy: "Stop the meter! I won't pay you anything for driving back and forth! I won't pay you at all!" Doggy, calm and collected as he is, absorbed this speech like a champ and told the queen: "Easy there, ma'am. The meter isn't even running yet." The woman then relented and said: "Oh, very well. I will drive with you then. Take

---

[86] *"Haista paskaa sä saatana homo!"* – *"Fuck you, you fucking faggot!"* in Finnish slang. *"Sniff some shit, you fucking faggot!"* in direct translation.

me to Sports." It's a sports bar in Matinkylä, where I have picked up "interesting" clients myself.

Doggy started driving. After a minute she started screaming again: "Wow, does your meter go or what? We just started driving and it's already showing 9 euros!" Doggy then told the client: "Of course it's showing that, it's after 8pm and the cost of starting a drive is 8.80." She kept at it: "I'm not paying for this drive!"

Hearing that, Doggy stopped the car in the middle of the street, about 300m before the bar and asked her: "Are you paying or not?" "No," the biddy answered and tried to exit the car and flee.

As she was in a hurry, her foot got stuck between the seat and the floor of the car – her shoe came off and fell back into the car. She wasn't discouraged though – she went across street walking in a hurry, towards the bar when she suddenly changed her mind. She turned around and came back to the taxi. In addition to getting her shoe back she had something important say to Doggy. The Finnish gal yelled to the Finnish-Swedish Doggy: *"Haista paskaa, sä saatana homo!"* At the same time she grabbed her shoe from the car and limped away, even her skirt was on crooked.

Doggy then cancelled the fare and drove off.

> "I will cut your throat if you start fucking with me too much."

A driver that Doggy knew once picked up a guy from a post in **southern Espoo**. The fare wanted to go to **Lepppävaara** train station. On the way, a few kilometers from the post towards Leppävaara the guy spilled his beer. The driver told the client: "You have to pay for the cleaning because I can't work with a car like this." The client agreed with the proposition.

When they were on the **Turunväylä** highway, just a few kilometers from Leppävaara, the bastard in the back seat had opened a can of energy drink. The energy drink had splashed out of the can and the contents were again on the seat and floor. To that, the taxi driver stopped the car and told the scumbag: "Throw the can out of the car! You just spilled your beer, now you're doing the same with your energy drink." The scumbag answered: "Hey, I have been in prison for ten years. I have a knife with me. If you start fucking with me, I'll cut your fucking throat!" The driver just answered, "Uhuh" to that and continued driving to the Leppävaara post. When they arrived he asked for help from the other drivers, because there was a madman out of control in his car. The scumbag escaped the car, as he saw the plan through. The drivers pursued him but decided to let him go after he had sprayed tear gas in the faces of his followers...

Just like that, he was gone for the night, without paying the bill. Later the police got him though.

## Half a kilo of coke, three drunk business men and a broken navigation system

It was an uplifting Friday evening in **January**. No clouds in the sky, the stars were shining like reflectors in a dark blue ceiling. About half a meter of snow was on the ground, if not more. The temperature was winter-like, dropping to -20 degrees Celsius at night.

Work-wise, it was pretty calm until midnight. There were clients, a bit of driving but nothing crazy.

While driving towards **Kauklahti** in **southwest Espoo**, I thought I would drive my round until I had the next hundred in my register. I was missing about 20 euros. I just needed one *keikka*[87] to finish my round.

I noticed on Data that there was a fare in Kauklahti. It had been there for a while, ordered about half an

---

[87] *Keikka - a chariot in Finnish. It is also meant as a tour or a concert tour in slang. Taxi drivers usually mean it as a fare.*

hour earlier. I decided to take the fare since I was driving there anyway.

I took it. I entered the address to the navigation system and saw that I "only" had about 12 kilometers to go.

I don't know how the navigation system directed me but soon the 12 kilometers had become 19. It turned out that the client was in **Gumböle**[88] not in Kauklahti. About a 7 kilometers difference.

I arrived the correct spot in Gumböle – on a dark forest road, a few houses. Fortunately the client had already exited the house so we found each other easily.

The customer was about 25 years old, a bit chubby and had glasses. He wanted to go from his friend's house to **Järvenperä**[89], another place in the middle of nowhere. I had to drive about 10 kilometers northeast. The guy was silent and calm and we had no problems driving with him.

I took the man from Gumböle to Järvenperä and decided to drive south, back to **Kivenlahti**, my

---

[88]*Gumböle - a district of western Espoo. It is located about 25km west of Helsinki.*
[89]*Järvenperä - a district of Mid-Espoo. It is located about 25km to the northwest of Helsinki.*

"home". It's closer to civilization and safer than driving in the woods of Järvenperä or Gumböle. On the way, about 6 kilometers away, was the **Espoo center** where it was more than likely to find another client.

About 3 kilometers from the Espoo center I got a new fare. It was from **...tie** street. My boss had mentioned some time ago never to take a customer from that address but I had not remembered that at 6 am.

I took the fare, thinking to myself that it was probably some old lady trying to get on a train, bus or a nursing home.

Arriving at the destination I saw a one-story building with a gable roof and barred windows made from bricks. It was like a little shop from the 80s.

I stopped in front of the house, in a yard with gravel, about 6-7 meters from the front door. There was no movement for the first few minutes. I was just about to leave when I saw someone waving to me from the door. I didn't see exactly who it was. So I waited for a few more minutes until two quite chubby guys and a smaller guy came. The trio was drunk, naturally, and properly drunk. I was thinking to myself "shit, this *keikka* is what I needed. I just had to take ONE more. Well now I got it".

The men came out of the hut one by one and tottered to my car. One big guy and his smaller friend got in the back and the other big guy sat in the front seat. With them the car was instantly filled with stupid conversation and the stench of alcohol.

When I asked where they would like to go, they said **Viherlaakso**, which was about 5 kilometers to the east. "Shit, this is just what I needed – to go on an adventure in the middle of fucking nowhere – to end my round," I thought to myself again.

On the way to Viherlaakso the company reconsidered and decided to go to **Tammisto**[90] district in **Vantaa** (about 20 kilometers to the northeast). I had no idea where it was. When asking the guys for the exact address, no one knew – they just told me to drive to Vantaa, towards **Tikkurila**. "Sorry guys, I'm just a beginner, maybe you can guide me. Even better if you could give me the address," I explained to them.

They gave me the address and the navigation system told me that the destination was 17 kilometers away. The beginning of this fare gave me a funny feeling that this was going to be an interesting drive. And it was.

---

[90]***Tammisto*** *– a district of Vantaa. It's located about 20km northeast of Helsinki.*

The fellows promised a big tip if I took them there. They were talking about hundreds of euros. I didn't make much of it because it sounded ridiculous. I just thought: *yeah-yeah, just some big mouths.*

After an annoyingly loud trip we were turning off **Kehä III** to **Myyrmäki**, a district of Vantaa, my navigation system decided to die. It had happened before but not like this – early in the morning with this kind of company in this kind of place. I had 5-6 kilometers still to go.

I asked the guys, disturbing their "intellectual" conversation, if someone could give me directions, that the navigation system had died. Nobody heard me. I turned the volume way up and yelled to the drunken company "HELLLOOOO?! Does someone know if we should take this exit or continue on this road?"

To that, the loud conversation stopped. Every man was trying to see through the frozen window where we were exactly to answer me. One fellow then asked, "Where are we anyway?" All I could tell them was, "On Kehä III but does somebody know where to go?" The car was quiet for a moment and then the guys started discussing where they could be.

Since I had just missed the Myyrmäki exit sign, nobody knew where we were and how should we continue. One of the fellows proposed to drive ahead, another one didn't quite agree with that plan and thought that we should have turned to Myyrmäki. The third guy didn't have any ideas.

14. A part of Kehä III motorway.

I stopped the car at a roundabout after the exit and announced resolutely: "I am not driving anywhere until someone gives me directions." The discussion continued if we should drive ahead or turn back or take the exit. Nobody had any idea where we were. It was -25 degrees and a few meters of snow outside and everything was just white all around us. All I could say between their discussion was "We had a deal that you would tell me where to go but now we're fucked."

The big guy in the backseat thought that the big guy in the front should have directed me the whole time. This guy just laughed and said, "I have no idea how to get to ...tie street." To that, the third, a little guy, looking through the back windows and carefully evaluating the situation, had an idea that I should make a U-turn. In the middle of the highway. I asked, "How should I do that, being on the highway with four driving lanes and a metal bar separating the opposing lanes?" He realized that it would be pretty complicated to pull that off. He then suggested driving until we got to a hotel. I asked if he knew of a hotel and where. He didn't know for sure but thought there was bound to be a hotel somewhere. I said, "Maybe there's one in the next 100 kilometers but we're not going to drive that far."

The guy sitting next to me decided that he would like some beer in this situation. The other big fellow then commented that they hadn't got any beer but a bit of cocaine wouldn't be bad until we figured out where to go.

After he finished his sentence, he pulled a baggie full of cocaine out from somewhere and asked me if I wanted some too. I turned around to see what the guy was doing and if he really had cocaine. To my surprise, he did. The man had a baggie of about half a kilo of white powder, ...

*You can read the end of the story in "Part Two".*

15. A map of Finland, showing its neighbors. [91]

---

[91]*Sources used:*

http://www.stat.fi/tup/suoluk/suoluk_vaesto_en.html
http://www.stat.fi/tup/suoluk/suoluk_vaesto_en.html#region
http://finland.fi/Public/default.aspx?contentid=160032&nodeid=44491&culture=en-US

# APPENDIX

## A brief introduction to Finland. The area, number of citizens, bigger cities

Because the book contains many names of places, I decided to add some notes about Finland here before continuing.

At the end of 2013, Finland had a population of **5.45 million** people: 2.68 million men and 2.77 million women. There were 706 people who were more than 100 years old: 89 men and 617 women. Nationalities were divided between **Finnish (89%), Swedish (5.34%), Sami (0.04%), Russians (1.22%) and other nationalities (4.09%)**. A total of 47.7% of those people are single, 37% married and 15.3% divorced. There were **44,700 Estonians, 30,700 Russians, 8,300 Swedes and 7,400 Somalians** immigrated to Finland at the end of 2013. There are 3.48 million people between the ages 15-69. It's interesting that in the year 1900, there were 2.65 million people in Finland. So in 113 years the population of Finland has more than doubled.

The bigger cities by population are **Helsinki (612,600), Espoo (260,700),** Tampere (220,400) and Vantaa (208,000).

**The size of Finland as of January 1, 2014 338,424km$^2$,** so almost seven times as big as its southern neighbor Estonia. For comparison, Finland is bigger than the United Kingdom, which is "only" 229,848km$^2$. Finland is the fifth biggest country in Western Europe. Its length from north to south is **1160km** and width from west to east is **540km.**

The largest areas in Finland are **Lapland (92,660km$^2$), North Ostrobothnia (35,508km$^2$)** and **Kainuu (21,500km$^2$).**

The biggest cities in southern Finland by area are Helsinki, Espoo and Vantaa.

## Official languages, climate, primary export

The official languages in Finland are **Finnish** and **Swedish**.

Finland became independent on **December 6, 1917,** after being part of the Russian Empire for 108 years before that and a part of Sweden for 600 years before that.

The climate in Finland is very contrasty. In 2013 the lowest measured temperature was in Sodankylä,- **39.7 degrees Celsius**. The highest temperature in the same year was measured in Liperi, **+32.4 degrees Celsius**.

**The main export articles in Finland are** electronics, metal, machinery, wood and paper, chemicals.


### The bigger cities in southern Finland

**Helsinki**[92]

The city of Helsinki was built by the order of the King of Sweden, **Kustav Vaasa** on the delta of the river Vantaanjoki in **1550. In 1643** the city arose in its current location. It was named the capital of independent Finland in **1917.**

There were **612,000** people living in **Helsinki as of January 1, 2014.** The city covers an area of **719km$^2$**, of which 503km$^2$ is underwater and 216km$^2$ on the land. There is 123km of coastline in Helsinki. There are 315 islands in the area of Helsinki. The annual average temperature is 5.9 degrees Celsius. The

---

[92]*Sources used:* http://www.visithelsinki.fi/en

hottest month is July when it is an average of 17.7 degrees Celsius and the coldest is February (-6.8 degrees Celsius).

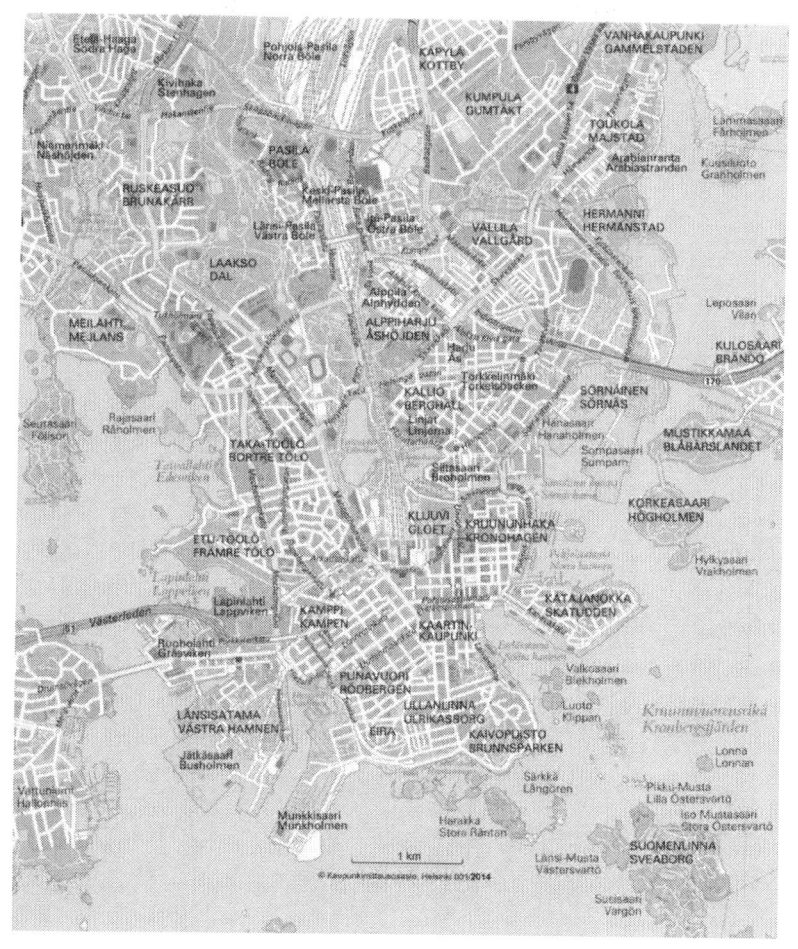

16. Map of the center of Helsinki with its nearest districts.

## Espoo[93]

Espoo has been mentioned in history as early as the **14th century**, when the King's Road from **Turku** to **Viipuri** went through it. It became a small town in **1963** and in **1972** Espoo got its city rights. In **2008** Espoo celebrated its 550th anniversary.

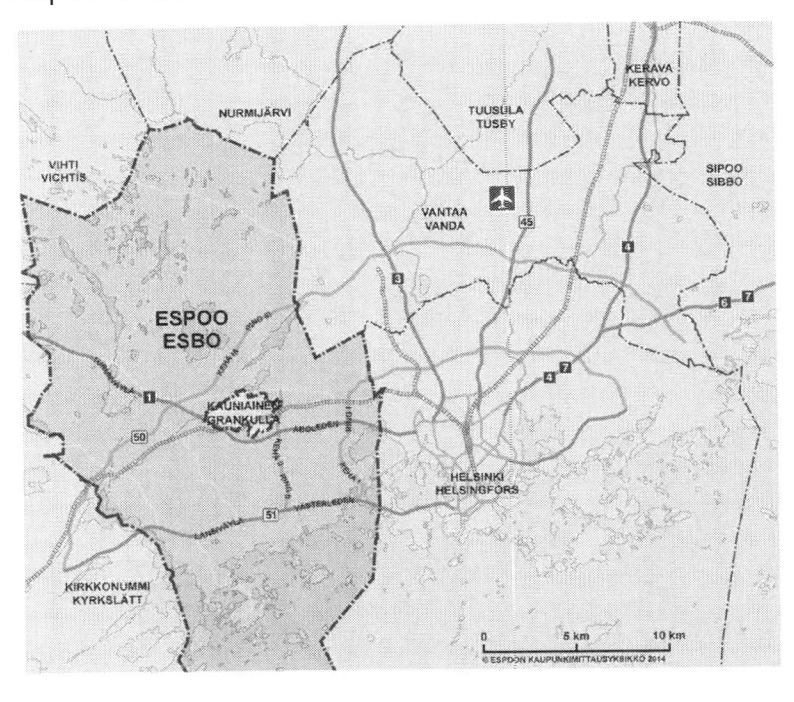

*17. Espoo and its nearest towns and bigger areas.*

The population of Espoo is 260,700 and it covers an area of 528km$^2$, of which 312km$^2$ is on land and bodies of water comprise 216km$^2$

---

[93]*Sources used:* http://www.visitespoo.fi/en/

Below is the map of the biggest cities in southern Finland. On the left you can see **Espoo, Helsinki** is below, on the right. To the north of Helsinki is **Vantaa**. **The Helsinki-Vantaa International Airport** is also located there.

**The bigger districts in Espoo are** (in random order)**: Leppävaara** (12km northeast of Helsinki), **Tapiola** (9km west of Helsinki), **Matinkylä-Olari** (14km west of Helsinki), **Espoonlahti** (18km west of Helsinki) and **Espoo center** (20km northwest of Helsinki).

Espoo also has smaller districts like **Otaniemi** (student town, 9km west of Helsinki), **Keilaniemi** (business and technology center, 8.5km west of Helsinki), **Westend** (10km west of Helsinki, on the coast of Finland), which is a rich neighborhood with only a few apartment houses. To the west, right next to Westend is **Haukilahti,** which mostly has big apartment buildings.

Just north of Matinkylä-Olari is a small business district, **Olarinluoma,** with many office buildings and car dealerships. To the west of Matinkylä, just next to Espoonlahti is **Kivenlahti** and just west of that a brand new neighborhood called **Saunalahti**. About 9km west from that is **Masala**. 10km west from that is a bigger center named **Kirkkonummi.**

*18. A yacht harbour in Haukilahti.*

I would also mention **Mankkaa**, which is next to Tapiola and Olarinluoma and between Tapiola-**Kilo**. Kilo itself is 13km northwest of Helsinki. Next to it is a bigger and richer neighborhood **Kauniainen**, which actually has its own city rights.

## Vantaa[94]

In 2013, about **208,000 people** were living in the 873km$^2$ area of **Vantaa**. The bigger districts are: **Ki-**

---

[94]*Used sources:* http://www.vantaa.fi/information_on_vantaa , http://www.vantaa.fi/instancedata/prime_product_julkaisu/vantaa/embeds/vantaawwwstructure/96754_Vantaa_General_information_EN_20052013.pdf

vistö, **Myyrmäki, Korso, Aviapolis, Tikkurila, Koivukylä, Hakunila.** Also there is the **Helsinki-Vantaa International airport**, about 18km of Helsinki.

For more details about Finland, go to the home page of the Finnish Statistics Department.


## Finnish taxis, ordering taxis and the taxi culture

Like you saw from the numbers in the last chapter, the working area and potential clientele of a taxi driver could be quite large. Especially the drivers who mostly drive in Espoo, Helsinki and Vantaa.

**The three towns cover an area of 1401km$^2$, containing about 15,000 streets and have about 1.1 million people.** Of course you can't compare the number of streets with New York or London, but it's still a notable number for a taxi driver to learn.

It is estimated, there are about **5,000 regularly working taxi drivers.** Adding to that, there are about 4,000 drivers who drive taxis after their day jobs.

The quality of the taxis used in Finland is mostly high. The cars in use have to be switched out every 3 years by law. The cleanliness and quality of the trip vary because of the different drivers. It's rare that a taxi is dirty from the inside, because in Finland, it is forbidden to smoke, eat and drink in a taxi. The latter two don't count for the driver of course. If you wish to eat or drink in a taxi yourself, I advise you to ask permission, just to be polite.

**The starting fee and the kilometer charge are the same all over the country.** The starting fee is 5.90 euros on workdays (6 am to 8) and Saturdays (6 am to 4 pm.). On holidays or Sundays the fee is 9 euros around the clock.

**The kilometer charge depends on the number of people using the taxi.** If there are 1-2 passengers, the charge is 1.52 euros. If there are 3-4 passengers, it's 1.86 euros.

If you pre-order the taxi, **the extra cost is 7euros.** Pre-ordering the taxi does not guarantee that the taxi will be there at the time you need it to be. For example, on weekends during the night and early mornings you might not get your pre-ordered taxi because of the number of people moving around the city going partying or coming back home. On weekdays it is not a problem.

I recommend ALWAYS taking **the receipt** when you finish your ride and pay your bill. If you leave your personal belongings in the car, the receipt has all the information about the driver and car, so it's easy to contact the driver or the employer. Also, you can use the information if you have had problems with the trip or the driver.

If you wish to bring a bigger package or an animal with you, the driver has right to add a special fee for transporting "cargo." This is always not the situation, though. It depends on what kind of deal you can make with the taxi driver.

And of course you have to be able to pay **in cash or by card**. And again, make sure you take the receipt, PARTICULARLY if you're in an unsober state.

If you want to know how much taxi drivers get paid, then the stories of mystical salaries are legends. There is no base salary for a taxi driver in Finland. The driver only earns a percent of the money in the register. It's becoming harder to make a living by driving a taxi every year. Thus, a little tip is always welcome. There are too many taxis and not enough customers. One of the reasons is Finland's fast development of the public transport system, including the subway and the current economic crisis.

You got an idea of the real culture of using taxis in Finland through the previous stories. I hope your rides in Finnish taxis will go pass peacefully and comfortably. It depends mostly on you.

## WHICH IS IT – VIRO OR EESTI?

The question has gripped both nationalities for almost a century – which is the correct term for the Republic of Estonia? Is it *Viro* or *Eesti*? V*irolaiset* or *eestiläiset*?

With the permission of the Estonian Mother Tongue Society and the author of the article, Riho Grünthäl, I will publish some fragments of an article that talks about the topic. The article is called "Lauri Kettunen – the representative of the Estonian language in Finland." You can read the whole article here:

http://www.emakeeleselts.ee/esa/ESA_52_pdf/Grynthal.pdf


## Lauri Kettunen – the representative of the Estonian language in Finland

Note: The purpose of this article is to reveal Lauri Kettunen's attitude towards Estonia and the Estonian language after his return from Tartu to Helsinki in the 1920s and 1930s. Because of his certain and relentless views he was constantly in conflict with the Finnish and Estonian language scholars of the time.

Keywords: Lauri Kettunen, the history of the Estonian language, the Estonian language in Finland, the tribal movement

The shelves of research libraries, research bibliographies and electronic databases confirm that the professor of the languages of the Baltic Sea at the universities of Tartu and Helsinki, Lauri Kettunen, was an exceptional scholar. His interests were much more wider than the scientists at the time and even later. If you take into consideration that the material he collected is indispensable to the research of the languages of the Baltic Sea, it is surprising that his life work has been mentioned so rarely.

...

### E.A. Tunkelo

One of the culminations of Kettunen's debate was the argument with E. A. Tunkelo, the long-time editor in chief of *Virittäjä* in 1929. The result was the resignation of Kettunen from *Virittäjä*. The debate was about the topic, which has also been argued about later – is it right to use the name *Eesti* or *Viro* in the Finnish language.

You can read Kettunen's opinion about in the textbook, which came out in 1926, which presented the differences in the Finnish and Estonian languages. So it was a few years before the public debate. Kettunen was certain and relentless about his opinion that the only correct term is *Eesti*.

As he published extensive research about the ethnonyms of *Viro* and *Vironmaa*, Tunkelo (1929) probably didn't expect such a stormy response to the article. But he had picked a topic which was awkward, the question of calling Finnish southern neighbors *Eesti* or *Viro* awakened strong emotions. After the collision of Kettunen and Tunkelo, there wasn't any hope of solving the debate calmly[95].

Tunkelo's article is long and comprehensive, an historical and semantic overview about the names used describing *Viro* and *Vironmaa*. He had researched a large number of historical sources, which had documented the history of Estonia and *Virumaa* since the 16th century. Because the control over the

---

[95] *The question of using* Viro *or* Eesti *has been debated several times during the last few decades. The reason usually is that Estonians call their country* Eesti *and their language the Estonian language. The natural debate on the topic of* Viro *or* Eesti *has been complicated even to the generations after Kettunen. The question upset a lecturer who had been teaching the Estonian language in the University of Helsinki for 25 years, Eeva Niinivaara. On her 85th birthday in 1986, along with Otto Aho, she confirmed that president Kekkonen had forced people to take the name* Viro *to use. Otto Aho was known for introducing and translating the tribal literature after the war. Eeva Niinivaara and Otto Aho were part of a small group who celebrated the independence day of Estonia in Finland during the 1950s until 1980s, when the tribal theme disappeared.*

land constantly changed during the centuries, the political borders changed also. Tunkelo demonstrates in chronological order how the name Viro was used during the Swedish occupation in Finnish texts and how the meaning of *Eestimaa* and *Liivimaa* changed during the Russian occupation. They had both become a name of the province.

Tunkelo's main point was that in the Finnish language, the name *Viro* meant the area of "*Viron herttuakuntta*" during the Swedish era in the 17th century (Tunkelo 1929a: 114-116). It covered the area of ethnographic Estonia at the time. The Republic of Estonia later came into existence in the same geographic area, known as *Viro* in the Finnish language. The last examples of the use of the word *Viro* are from when Estonia was already independent. Tunkelo cites Kettunen's Estonian textbook, where Kettunen uses the word *Viro* meaning "*Virumaa*." *Vironmaa* is as old as *Viro* in Tunkelo's view and he feels that it confirms that *Viro* could have been used to describe a larger area before the Swedish time (Tunkelo 1929: 124).

Tunkelo's conclusion was that the use of the word *Viro* in Finnish to describe "Estonia" is as logical as using the word *vaimo* to mean "woman," or of the Estonian word *valu* (pain) to mean *valo* (light) in Finnish.

For Kettunen (1929: 278), Tunkelo's article meant that for historical reasons, the aims of the tribal movements were being cancelled. In his references, he brings attention to the fact that the more important newspapers in Finland – *Helsingin Sanomat* and *Uusi Suomi* – had not been using the name *Eesti* and even the official speakers use *Viro* rather than *Eesti*. Estonians were against the name *Viro* for the same reasons as the Finnish were against the Karelians using *Ruotsi* to describe Finland and *ruotsalainen* to describe Finnish people.

*Heimoasia vaatii menestyäkseen sitä rakkautta, „joka ei omaansa etsi", vaan on valmis myös jotakin omastaan toiselle uhraamaan. Lieneekö ennenaikaista puhua sellaisesta heimorakkaudesta?*
(Kettunen 1929a: 278.)

Kettunen says that if they stopped using the name *Viro* and replaced it with the name *Eesti*, the Finns could satisfy the Estonian people's wishes.

Tunkelo (1929b) had nothing left to do than to respond to Kettunen, calmly weighing every possible way to take a better look at the topic. He cites examples and background information. He talks about the older history of the tribal movement and quotes a scholar-poet A.

Jännes (known as Arvid Genetz when talked about as a language scholar). Genetz was one of the first to experiment with ways to shorten the Estonian and Finnish language in the end of the 19th century:

*Eesti mä oon ja eestiksi jään, kunnekka kalma mun peittävi pään.*

The debate on languages of the tribal movement even touched on the topic of bringing words from the Estonian language to the Finnish language, because loans from the Finnish language do exist in Estonian. Even Genetz had come up with an idea to replace the words loaned from Indo-European languages (for example *preili* (lady), *müts* (hat) and *vorst* (sausage)) with words loaned from Finnish; and vice versa – replacing Finnish Indo-European loans (*säkki* (bag) or *synti* (sin)) with words from Estonian.

Tunkelo (1929b: 290) thinks that every language should loan as many words from other languages as needed. His decision is clear: if you're talking about *Eesti* or *Viro*, there is a long list of reasons why you should use the latter. So the debate has ended for him.

## E. A. Saarimaa

...

Looking back, it's no wonder that Kettunen returned to his contacts from his time in Estonia and published his writings in Estonian and in Estonian Literature after leaving *Virittäjä*. The latter published his article that had been refused in *Virittäjä*, about the use of the names *Viro* and *Eesti* in Finnish (Kettunen 1931b).

Kettunen's dedication to his opinion was clear after he published an article called "*Voittava 'Eesti'*" in a magazine called *Suomalainen Suomi* in 1939 (Kettunen 1939).

Dear Reader,

Thank you for reading my book. I hope you liked it. If you did, please leave your positive comment or review.

If you would like to contact me, please e-mail me at Paul.V.Speed@gmail.com or comment on my blog: https://lifeinfinlanddotnet.wordpress.com/ .
Additionally you can find my stories on Facebook: https://www.facebook.com/RealLifeInFinland and Twitter: https://twitter.com/RealFinnishLife

*Sincerely yours*
*Paul V. Speed*

Printed in Great Britain
by Amazon